~~UN~~WORTHY

U̶N̶WORTHY

Society in Search of the Courage to Accept
Disability Through a Lens of Grace

JOSEPH ANKOMAH CROMWELL

Foreword by Dr. Sam Kabue

Inner City
PRESS
Houston, Texas

© Copyright 2019 by Joseph Ankomah Cromwell

All Rights Reserved. Without limiting the rights under the copyright reserved above, this book may not be reproduced, in whole or in part, stored in a retrieval system, or transmitted in any form or by any means (electronic, mechanical, photocopying, recording, or otherwise) except for brief quotations in critical reviews or publications without the prior permission of the publisher or author.

Disclaimer: The author has tried to recreate events, locales and conversations from his memories of them. In order to maintain their anonymity, in some instances the author has changed the names of the individuals and places. The author also may have changed some identifying characteristics and details such as physical properties, occupations and places of residence.

Worthy, Society in Search of the Courage to Accept Disability through a Lens of Grace, by Joseph Ankomah Cromwell

ISBN: 978-1-7323519-4-3 Paperback

Includes bibliographical references and index
1. Inclusion and Society   2. Christian Living   3. Title

Editor: E. Obeng-Amoako Edmonds
First Edition: 2017938652

Author's portrait picture: courtesy Andrews K. Mensah (Ayoo Photos)
+233244060681

Publisher: Ink City Press, Houston, Texas (USA)
Rights for publishing this work or in non-English languages are administered by Ink City Press or Magnolia Press, in partnership with Frontage Road Literary Agency, an Atlantic BG Media company. www.frlagency.com

To contact the author
Email: cromwellworthy@gmail.com or call (+233) 244 808975

It is comforting to note how the author, himself a person with disability, candidly discusses and brings to bear theological insights to the subject as it affects society in general. I highly recommend it for the reading public and encourage further interrogation of the subject matter by all manner of people who care.

— Very Rev. Dr. Sam Prempeh
A former Moderator of the Presbyterian Church of Ghana.

In *Worthy*, Rev Joseph Ankomah Cromwell has raised an extremely pertinent issue that should engage society's attention for a long time to come. In a disarming and engaging manner, the book touches on theological, cultural, and developmental perspectives of disability and how society's response has fallen far short of what it should be. This book should arouse righteous anger that leads to transformational action, particularly by the Christian Church. It's about time."

— Dr. Angela Dwamena-Aboagye
Lawyer, Theologian and Women and Mental Health Advocate.

Worthy will change your perspective of persons with disabilities forever. Rev. Joseph Cromwell does not only advocate that all people are worthy to serve community and the Lord, but he demonstrates this by his personal life. This book will cause you to humble yourself to accept your own 'hidden disabilities' and then show concern for other persons with disabilities in order to assist one another in this world. *Worthy* will help the church to spearhead the fight against discrimination of persons with disabilities and play a leading role in integrating them into mainstream church life and other aspects of life in general.

— Apostle Professor Opoku Onyinah
Past Chairman of the Church of Pentecost
Former President of Ghana Pentecostal and Charismatic Council

CONTENTS

Acknowledgement 1
Foreword 7
Introduction 13
Chapter 1: In the Potter's Hand 21
Chapter 2: Mud 33
Chapter 3: A Glimpse of Amazing Grace 45
Chapter 4: Sri Lanka 57
Chapter 5: A Culture in Search of a Heart 73
Chapter 6: Trading Places 83
Chapter 7: What Would Jesus Do? 91
Chapter 8: Different on Purpose 103
Chapter 9: Beyond the Guilt 117
Chapter 10: An Awakening 129
Chapter 11: Worthy 141
Chapter 12: Inside Out 151
Chapter 13: Saving Hands 161
Chapter 14: Turnaround 171
Chapter 15: Where Grace Lives 185
Chapter 16: Salt and Light 193
Chapter 17: Our Declaration 203
Chapter 18: Worth Fighting For 209
    Afterword 222
    Index 224
    References 235

ACKNOWLEDGEMENT

I thank the Almighty God for His grace and mercies that give life to the simplest of ideas that honor His name. I express my heartfelt gratitude to the Very Rev. Dr. Sam Prempeh, in whose tenure as Moderator of the Presbyterian Church of Ghana, I was commissioned into the ministry. His encouragement and mentorship have contributed a lot to my success as a minister of the gospel.

I further express my profound gratitude to the current Moderator, Rt. Rev. Prof. Joseph Obiri Yeboah Mante, and all my lecturers at the Trinity Theological Seminary, Legon-Accra, under whose nurture and tutelage I had my theological education. I am also grateful to my lecturers and supervisors at the University of Cape, most especially, Rev. Professor Emmanuel Adow Obeng, Rev. Professor Eric Anum and Rev. Professor Benjamin Abotchie Ntreh. Passing through their hands was like gold ore passing through the refinery; you come out glittering.

I owe a debt of gratitude to Rev. Professor Abraham Berinyuu, who introduced me to Ecumenical Disability Advocates Network (EDAN) of World Council of Churches; Mrs. Gertrude Oforiwaa Fefoame, co-member of EDAN, and Dr. Sam Kabue of Kenya (who graciously consented to write the Foreword) and Mrs. Anjeline Okola, also of Kenya (both had been Programme Coordinators at certain points in time for EDAN).

I thank my Director at the Ramseyer Training Centre, Rev. Gideon Puplampu, and my co-lecturers: Rev. Dr. Asiedu Amoako, Rev. Samuel Ampiaw, Rev. Dr. Brandford Yeboah, Rev. Dr. Eric Teye-Kau and Rev. Mrs. Afia Ban Asemiah for their enormous encouragement. I also thank the rest of the RTC staff and students on various programmes of the Centre.

I also acknowledge the academic counsel I have received recently from Prof. Musa W. Dube, Rev. Canon Prof. Noble Amanze, and Prof. Fidelis Nkonozana, all of the University of Botswana, encouraging me to do more to help draw in more people to discuss, reflect and theologize on disability issues. I also appreciate the effort of Dr. Angela Dwamena Aboagye, a Mental Health Advocate.

I am very grateful to Apostle Prof. Opoku Onyinah, past Chairman, Church of Pentecost, and Rev. Dr. Emmanuel Anim, Principal, Pentecost Theological Seminary (PTS), in Kasoa, Ghana for opening their doors to us (myself and Mrs. Gertrude Oforiwaa Fefoame), to develop, mount, and teach a course (i.e., *Disability and Theological Studies*) in their seminary. To all my students at PTS, I thank you for the encounters that have enriched my teaching and learning experiences, just as I hope they did yours. I am also grateful to Very Rev. Dr. Abedu Quarshie, who provided me a bigger platform to interact with all the Superintendent Ministers of the Methodist Church Ghana, and to take them through *"Ministering to persons with disabilities"* during SOCED 2017 at Kumasi.

I am thankful to Mr. and Mrs. Michael Farchie, and Rev. Mrs. Afia Ban Asemiah, for agreeing to proofread and review the manuscript, and to help make it *a must-read*.

I have a deep appreciation for Dr. Samuel Agyepong who has given me immense support, making sure I succeed in fulfilling my ministry. Also, I am grateful to Rev. and Mrs. Patrick Asare Ayesu, Rev. and Mrs. Walter Kpentey, Rev. and Mrs. George B. Appiah Korang, Rev. and Mrs. Seth Achia Addo, Mr. and Mrs. Philip Achen Sunil, Mr. and Mrs. Gilbert Odjidja, Mrs. and Mrs. Frank Opata, Mr. and Mrs. Kingsley Akuoko, Mr. and Mrs. Charles Nortey, Mr. and Mrs. Offei Palm, Mr. and Mrs. Ebenezer Ntony Bediako, Mr. and Mrs. David Kuka, Mr. and Mrs. Samuel Mante, Mr. and Mrs. Osei Agyei, Police Officer DSP Cephas Coffie, Mad. Juliana Sowah, Mad. Beatrice Ampadu, Mad. Beatrice Kumi, Mad. Harriet Mireku, Mad. Dora Vondee, Mad. Rose

Acknowledgement

Afriyiye, Mad. Joana Asante, Mr. Samuel Aboagye, Mr. Daniel Ansah, Mr. Raymond Akuffo - C.E.O. Ideas Banc, the Mantes, Very Rev. Prof. John Ekem, Rev. and Mrs. Acheampong, the Borloz sisters – Arlette and Yvonne of Switzerland and Mad. Comfort Asae and their siblings. These people and a lot more have supported my family and ministry in diverse ways. May God replenish their resources and bless them.

There were the huge contributions and the sacrifices made by my family, especially my parents, Mr. Joseph Oliver Cromwell, and Mrs. Joycetina Anyankwabea Cromwell (now deceased), my siblings, Janet, William (recently deceased), and Samuel. I'm very grateful to my dear wife, Comfort and the children, Justina, Dinah and Joseph. I doff my hat for them, for always encouraging me not to relent on my mission. I am also grateful to my nephews and nieces Daniel, Monica, George, and Dorothy, for their hardworking and selfless devotion to the family.

I cannot say enough "thank yous" to both my uncle and his wife, Mr. and Mrs. Kwesi Arhin, who once visited us after an unfortunate train accident, and urged me to share my experiences and testimony. My family is eternally grateful to God our maker, and His Son Jesus Christ, for bestowing grace and mercies on us, over and over again.

This book has seen the light of day thanks to my friend, E. Obeng-Amoako Edmonds, who has tirelessly complemented my effort by working assiduously to have this work edited and produced with the highest possible standards of quality. *Merci mon ami!*

It took many months of research and several rounds of reviews to turn this manuscript into a book, and I am truly thankful for all the circumstances under which I gained insight into this subject, and for the people whose paths I crossed along the way.

Rev. Joseph Ankomah Cromwell

wor·thy

ˈwərTHē/

adjective

Having sufficient worth or importance

FOREWORD

I was glad when Joseph Cromwell requested me to write a foreword for this book, which largely narrates his own story and the seeming prejudice, cultural attitudes and exclusion that persons with disabilities undergo in their families, among peers without disabilities and equally in church and society.

I associate myself with Joseph's experience, having gone through very similar situations as a person with disability. This is not the place to tell my story, since that is not what I have been requested to do, but this is a resource that challenges both society and the Church to be more inclusive and to break down the walls that divide us. I very much recommend it to the Church and community leadership as well as general society. However, in writing this foreword, I have taken a theologically reflective approach, and the Church as my basis in taking further a call to transformation, which is a major theme in this book.

The wonder of creation is the precision and diversity with which God has endowed the world. This diversity extends to the same specs including human creation–tall, short, male, female, blue eyes, brown eyes, non-disabled, disabled . . . The miracle of being human is that we are all individual, even when we are identical twins. We all have different strengths, limitations and preferences. Even though according to the standards of the world we are all unique, the Bible is clear in one thing: "We are all made in the image of God."

This needs to be a binding factor that plays down our seeming world view differences and to see each other as equal before God. However, society, and likewise the church, have considered some as being more different if not more equal than others, leading to the exclusion of some from social and spiritual life on the same bases with others. Most affected in this are persons with disabilities.

It is in this respect that I reflect from a disability perspective on the words of St. Paul: "Do not conform any longer to the pattern of this world but be transformed by the renewing of your mind. That you will be able to test and approve what God's will is—his good, pleasing and perfect will." (Romans 12: 2). It is a fact that the world has failed to see the outstretched arm of God which beckons us to transform the world to conform to what God's creation of humanity intended. Human creation has failed to live in accordance with the will of God.

We live in a world where values like physical fitness, beauty, wealth and power are upheld as the norm and those who do not meet these standards are ignored, marginalized and I would say despised. We have as a society found it too difficult to see the Christ who teaches a different gospel where the weak are strengthened, the last are made first, and the poor are exalted. The Church, which should be a ministry of inclusion, reconciliation and restoration finds it very hard to live up to its expectation. It has not exercised the love and compassionate virtues and values of Jesus Christ and thus has not followed its calling, which is to conform to his likeness as a minister of transformation.

Although Paul in Ephesians 2: 14 belabors the point that Christ came to break walls of division, we have remained divided along all forms of walls. These are walls which contradict Christ's ministry of reconciliation. Persons with disabilities, of whom I am one, remain isolated from mainstream society by walls of uneasiness on the part of others, walls of prejudice, walls of hatred, walls of competition, walls of fear, walls of ignorance, walls of theological prejudice and of cultural misunderstanding. Christ, in his seeming reversal of what the world considers the norm, calls the church to play the lead role of being an inclusive community, to tear down the walls.

Through his instructions to the Church in Rome as recorded in the Romans 12: 3-16 text titled *Gifts of Grace*, Paul describes the impact that living up to our faith should have on our characters and relationships with others. He says to them, "By the grace given to me I say to everyone among you not to think of himself more highly than he ought to think, but to think with sober judgment, each according to the measure of faith that God has assigned." (Romans 12:3).

Transformation begins with the awareness that God is in the center of all life. Transformation of our hearts will lead to the transformation of our attitudes and assumptions and this will lead to the healing of the community and of the earth. Its manifestation will be respect for all human beings. A prevailing attitude today is that people with disabilities are seen as weak and because of that, they need care.

As a result, they are viewed as objects of charity–those who receive what other persons give. They have themselves nothing to give. Thus, the persons with disability cannot meet other people in the churches on equal terms. They are regarded as somehow less than fully human. Even where a measure of acceptance has been achieved, they are accepted as the weaker parts of the body. This raises a question, "Is language of plurality not more adequate?"

To live with a disability is to live with other abilities and limitations that others do not have. All human beings live with limitations. Is not disability something that God has created in order to build a plural, and richer, world? How else can we interpret the word of God when he says to Moses "Who gave man his mouth? Who makes him deaf or dumb? Who gives him sight or makes him blind? Is it not I the Lord? Now go. I will help you speak and will teach you what to say." (Exodus 4:11).

When the Bible says that we are all created in the image of God, the disabled tend to be excluded from the "all" by practice and attitude. The image of God, which we bear, is that of creativity, relations or communion with one another and love for one another. The attitude to people with disabilities seems to exclude them from these values. Where they are upheld, it is the exception rather than the norm. In most cases, their presence is seen to overturn the order of things. They are seen as a negation of God's intention. Paul is calling on us to be transformed from these attitudes and to leave interdependent lives, respecting one another.

Respect for others has to begin with the acknowledgement of Paul's admonition that "So we, though many, are one body in Christ, and individually members one of another." (Romans 12:5). If this is going to be the reality in our life as a Church, the Church in this respect is a community of people with different yet complementary gifts.

Paul is very clear in his teaching that we complete each other and in the body of Christ through the gifts and talents of all people. He says in Romans 12:6: "Having gifts that differ according to the grace given to us, let us use them . . ." We have to use them to the uttermost of our giftedness, not just for ourselves, but also for the good of the body of Christ. He provides a list of examples of gifts and how we should use them: prophecy, service, teaching, exhortation, generosity, leadership and acts of mercy. He reminds us elsewhere: "For as in one body we have many members, and not all members have the same function, so we, though we are many, are one body in Christ, and individually we are members one of another . . ." (1 Cor.12: 12). Bringing together our gifts and talents is a vision of wholeness as well as of healing, of caring and of sharing at once. Just as the body is one and has many members, so it is with Christ.

However, even with all these gifts and the opportunity to exercise them, there are some underlying guiding principles in our Christian life and ministry. On top of the list is love for one another. He says in Rom. 12, verse 10: "Love one another with brotherly affection. Outdo one another in showing honor." We could be serving each other with our gifts just as a duty and as a craving to be seen as a church or a body of Christ. Service is not enough. It has to be given in love and concern.

We are also called upon to serve the Lord with zeal, to rejoice in hope, to be patient in tribulation, to be constant in prayer, to contribute to the needs of the saints and seek to show hospitality (Romans 12:11-13).

Finally, we are reminded to live in harmony with one another, not to be haughty, but to associate with the lowly. We all accept and proclaim that this is what the Church is and stands for. It is the basis of our unity as Christians. Transformation calls for the recognition of our interdependence and therefore our need for one another. God wills the acceptance and inclusion of each in a community of interdependence where each supports and builds up the other, and where each lives life to the fullest according to his circumstances and to the glory of God.

As St. Paul says, the parts of the body which seem to be weaker (we should notice that he does not say "actually are weaker") are indispensable (1 Cor. 12:22). It is a fact that disabilities impose limitations, sometimes more intensive than at other times. However, these limitations are a reminder of our need for interdependence. They are also a reminder of everyone's vulnerability, and therefore the need to rely not on our strength but on God's, to access his grace to sustain us. Living in this interdependence opens us to one another and to a deeper, more honest self-knowledge, and so makes us each more fully human, more fully people of communion, more fully realizing the image of God which we bear.

Interdependence is the key here. Even though the secular world stresses independence, we are called to live as a community dependent on God and on one another. No one of us should be considered a burden for the rest; and no one of us is simply a burden-bearer. "We all bear one another's burdens in order to fulfil the law of Christ" (Gal. 6:2).

Those of us who have disabilities need to take heart. Our conditions, imperfectness in accordance to the world standards, sickness or even disabilities should never be allowed to stand between us and service to the Lord. The world will discourage us on this account, but the Lord will have answers to our seeming or apparent weaknesses.

Paul's story in 2 Corinthians 12:7-9 is the best illustration. Despite his mighty work of preaching, teaching, healing and even raising people from the dead, he could have been discouraged by his own problem which he calls "a thorn in the flesh." In his wisdom and wishes, he would have wanted to be fit, perfect and healthy to serve God better. It took him a revelation to realize that his constant reminder of God's strength and its manifestations was this particular problem. Living and serving with it reminded him that God was not limited. Who then are we to observe other people's seeming or apparent weaknesses and to make a judgment on their fitness in serving the Lord? Who then are we to segment the body of Christ into weak and strong, perfect and imperfect, disabled or not disabled?

In our attitudes and actions towards one another, at all times, the guiding principle must be the conviction that we are incomplete, we are less than whole, without the gifts and talents of all people. We are not a full community without one another. Responding to and fully including people with disabilities is not an option for the Churches of Christ; it is the Church's defining characteristic.

Dr. Samuel Kabue,
Former Executive Secretary,
Ecumenical Disability Advocates Network
(A Programme of the World Council of Churches)

Member, United Nations Committee
of Experts on the Rights of Persons with Disabilities
31 May 2019

INTRODUCTION

It was 7 April 2017. My uncle, Mr. Kwesi Arhin and his wife, Auntie Esther, visited my family when they heard of a train accident we'd been involved in, on one unassuming morning. I narrated the ordeal to him and how I was convinced it was only God's unending grace that miraculously saved us unscathed. He remarked, "Write a book out of it, and I will proofread it for you." I smiled. Jovially, he even gave the title of the book as, "Escaped Like a Bird." It was a beautiful idea then, and I started giving it a thought to see how I would make it a reality. In all this, one thing became clear to me – the *time to start writing had arrived*.

Having two manuscripts already in waiting, one being my Master's thesis, *The Story of the Congenital Blind Man (John 9:1-41) and the Presbyterian Church of Ghana's Dealing with Disability*, and the other, a long essay I presented for my Bachelor of Divinity degree, *Two Theologians of Significance in Africa: Rev. Prof. Kwame Bediako & Prof. Mercy Amba Oduyoye*, I began the journey.

As I rummaged through the pages of many reference documents, and particularly the Word of God, so much of how society addressed the subject of disability stood out even more strongly for me. Gradually, what were to become the real contents of this book emerged–a whole lot of rich untold stories that would undeniably be of great value to a world in search of hope and eager for the reassurance of God's grace.

That little idea dropped into my mind by my uncle found its place in a larger space as I discussed disability as perceived throughout Africa and the world, to help create awareness of the ordeals persons with disabilities go through daily, and help find remedies for them. The message of Christ's matchless love for the world is that His finished work at

Calvary gives every one of us our identity. The true–and intended–title of the book is "*Worthy.*"

Conversely, society offers–consciously or otherwise–a platform for us to label one another as unworthy. The social backdrops in which this reality takes place elicit a strikingly different presentation. All along, it had been my heart's desire to find a common platform where the academia and non-academia would come together to deliberate, discuss, and help remove barriers and labels that limit the participation of persons with disabilities in their own environments and communities. *Worthy* seeks to provide that platform for common engagement, and at the end of the day, will see disability put in its proper perspective, devoid of derogatory tags and utter exclusion.

Worthy hinges mainly on an inspiration taken from a Bible story of the congenitally blind man in John 9:1-41, whose interaction with Jesus Christ captivated the society around him, no less the religious leaders in the region. The word "congenital" describes a condition, disease or physical abnormality that is present from birth, and he was an individual stuck with a label with which he would have to walk through life.

While his encounter and confessions were destined to be unforgettable through history, I can imagine a world where none of the people around him could have thought that his story would, fortunately, resonate in many communities around the world, and be told many centuries later. I have taken great inspiration from this man who refused to be intimidated by his own neighbors and religious leaders, to share my story as an open invitation to the general populace, to do further and deeper reflections on the subject of disability.

In *Worthy*, I have tried to look at disability issues from two main perspectives–from the disability and the non-disability perspectives, to give my readers a fair representation of the issues raised. While I have disabilities in walking and in speech, many of the people with whom my paths crossed did not have any (as far as my judgment will allow), yet their thoughts on disability would not let them sit on the fence without contributing to better our world with every opportunity at their disposal. The underlying belief remains that disability is universal, and together, we can all embrace one another's plight, share the challenges, and find pragmatic solutions to some of the gaps our world often unconsciously carves. Never again should we leave persons with disabilities to their own fate. Many share the opinion that society can do better for persons with disabilities, and if that is pursued honestly, many persons with disabilities can get along in life unhindered.

In the work itself, I have tried to recollect and tell many personal stories which bothered me on the issues I have been through as a person with disabilities. The more I delved into the stories, the more I wondered how much our society has learned–or not learned–from biblical truths. These stories may be disabling in their selves, but I have also seen them as "tools of empowerment" that can help uplift one from the doldrums of pity. On some occasions, I have also combined the stories with Bible stories and those of other people, in my modest hope to have provided my readers the opportunity to hear the empowering stories change communities and render them devoid of malice and discrimination.

In *Worthy*, I have also raised theological issues regarding the participation of persons with disability in the church's life. Over the years, the church's approach to disability has mainly been restrictive. For instance, ordination is seen to be a restricted area for persons with disabilities, and the structure and infrastructure also serve as barriers that limit the religious experience of such persons.

I am confident these stories can prompt us in contemporary society to confront the challenges that need to be dealt with. The years have changed, but our attitudes towards one another, unfortunately, have remained the same. The facts of the blind man's story are as relevant in our society as they were in his. To bring to the attention of the entire world the struggles, challenges, exclusion, stereotyping, and superstitions that persons with disabilities go through, I have been fortunate to be able to share my story. Some of my own experiences have a close affinity with the story of the blind man, and the underlying challenge remains the same. Again, these stories told, I believe, will encourage all of us to press on to deal with hindrances in life, as we battle to make our society a better place for all.

If Jesus left one mark through his meeting with the blind man, it would have been that regardless of who we are, and what mental or physical condition we are confronted with, all of us are worthy.

¹ As he went along, he saw a man blind from birth.
² His disciples asked him,
"Rabbi, who sinned, this man or his parents,
that he was born blind?"
³ "Neither this man nor his parents sinned," said Jesus,
"but this happened so that the works of God might be
displayed in him.

John 9: 1-3 New International Version (NIV)

Dedicated to my dear parents
Mr. Joseph Oliver Cromwell and Mrs. Joycetina Anyankwabea Cromwell
who defied all odds to get me educated.
I owe them a huge debt of gratitude.

CHAPTER

1

IN THE POTTER'S HANDS

Unexpected Moments, Unforeseen Hope

Jesus answered, "It was not that this man sinned, or his parents, but that the works of God might be made manifest in him." John 9:3

"You were two years old when you got paralyzed," Sisi told me.

Until then, my life as a toddler, I learnt, had not been any different from any other boy's in the small Okorase village where I grew up. The memories of the beautiful landscapes surrounded by the thick green forests remain just as fresh as my mother's voice calling out my name in the open sun on the bright afternoons.

The village was near the Koforidua Municipality, in Ghana's Eastern Region, tucked away in the serene fields. We occasionally stood by and watched the small minivans and other cars driving on that stretch of road to Accra, the nation's capital. As children, we would create our own games, including one where we used the license plates of the passing vehicles to play a game of chance. I watched the older boys and girls choose their favorite cars, and laugh over whose choice of vehicles and license number plates never seemed to turn the corner. After a time in the sun, we would run home.

There were other days when we would run to the roadside and sit there patiently, enjoying watching the cars passing. We would set a time, say about one hour, and within that time, each person would be tallying the number of vehicles that would be passing in his or her favor. When the time expired, the one with the highest tally would be the winner. There was no skill involved in the game, and there was no way to anticipate what was heading one's way. The outcome was entirely out of our hands. But the anticipation taught us a simple lesson in hope, that even something beyond our control had every power to bring a smile.

For much of my young life, it looked as if everything we would ever want to see in life was right there, an unassuming life filled with simple joy. Life in Okorase was innocent, and the challenges of the real world were very far away.

Okorase enjoyed a calm environment. The beautiful River Asuoyaa ran through my village and joined the River Densu. On our free days, we would spend much of our afternoons till dusk near the river in search of crabs and shellfish.

But there was an old woman in the village, Madam Ayorkor, (a.k.a. Mena Ayorkor) whose cottage was close to the river, who seemed to be overly protective of every child because she feared that one might drown if we kept playing in the river without any adult supervision. There was not any tragedy to endorse her worry, but her frown alone spelled her displeasure. Still, life was beautiful just as much as it was carefree.

I remember how sometimes as children in the neighborhood, we had to cross the river on our way to and back from school, and couldn't wait to dip our feet into the shallow parts of the river, while I would be carried at the back of one of my elder siblings. We looked around and admired the beauty of the cocoa trees and the green vegetation along the banks of the River Asuoyaa, majestic and strong. All it took was one fateful day to change the world I had known.

The mentioning of Madam Ayorkor brings to mind her brother, Papa Yaw Boahene. This man, together with Papa Yaw Kwei, Papa Asa Kwabena, Papa Kofi Boye, and Papa Oddoi, were conscripted into the West African Frontier Force that fought on the side of the British during the Second World War. They were taken to India to fight for the British, and had come back unscathed, though some of their colleagues suffered casualties and also lost their lives. Papa Asa Kwabena and Papa Kofi Boye were my direct relatives, and on moonlit nights, we would gather around them as they told us stories and shared their experiences with us.

During Independence Day celebrations, they would be in their outfits decorated with medals and would be marching to the delight of all. These veterans would at times chant wars songs from evening to deep into the night. I remember that the lyrics of one of the songs went like this:

> *Minnim baabi a mewu mada*
> (I don't know where I will die)
> *Minnim baabi a mewu mada*
> (I don't know where I will die)
> *Company Ɔtamfo Ɔbonsam*
> (Company, Satan, the enemy)
> *Menenam mu saa mayƐ basaa*
> (I have been a worried wanderer)
> *huwƐ nea mawie*
> (Look at my end)
> *menenam India, Burma, Congo*
> (I wander in India, Burma, Congo)
> *Minnim baabi a mewu mada*
> (I don't know where I will die).

Everybody in the village knew how to chant this song, and we held our veterans in very high esteem. By the year 2006, all of them had died, and now their memories have become very faint in the village. But as a nation, we cannot talk about our independence from the British Colonial Government without mentioning the huge contribution and sacrifices these veterans made.

On 28 February, 1948, three of them, Sergeant Cornelius Francis Adjetey, Lance Corporal Patrick Gagbale Attipoe, and Private Odartey Lamptey, were shot and killed, when they were marching to the seat of the British Colonial Government then at Christiansburg Castle, Osu-Accra, to demand fulfillment of the promises made to them before the war to help better their living conditions. Their death, however, became a catalyst to the struggle for Ghana's independence which had by then started. On 6 March, 1957, Ghana gained independence. Each year on 28 February, parades are held at the National and Regional capitals to remember the fallen heroes at Christiansburg Castle Crossroad Shootings.

A bronze statue in honor of Corporal Attipoe, standing in Kpota, Anyako, his hometown, in the Volta Region of Ghana, had this inscription underneath it:

> *In memory of Corporal Gagbale Attipoe who was the first of three gallant ex-servicemen who lost their lives at the 28th February, 1948 Christianborg Crossing Shooting Incident, a pivotal moment in Ghana's march to Independence. May this monument be a testament to your bravery and that of your comrades Sergeant Adjetey and Private Odartey Lamptey, Rest in peace.*

Indeed may the souls of the World War II Veterans (including those from my village, Okorase) rest in peace!

I fell ill just after I turned two, so I was later told, and my mother took me to a nearby hospital. She recalled that afternoon when a nurse gave me an injection, and it was much like any routine visit to the hospital at the time. Unfortunately, I came out of the hospital much different than I had entered, though the change went unnoticed until some few days later.

Since I was so young, I do not remember anything about the hospital or the incident where I received the injection, and certainly, have no way of recalling the name of the doctor or nurse. That person may have given me the same injection they gave many times to many other children in the area, except that after that day, I could never walk on my two feet again. That was the day I became paralyzed, and my life took a drastic turn.

I was too young to imagine what would become of the rest of my life. Somehow, I can imagine my parents trying to find a reason to believe in God's perfect character, and think that God still had me in His palms the entire way. As parents, they looked forward to the day that this discomfort would go away, and when my life would be back to how they had earlier known it to be.

My parents prayed. They wished I would be well quickly, so I could run up and down the hills with the boys and jump with them into the River Asuoyaa on the hot afternoons. They prayed more, but my condition did not improve. They took me to every hospital in the region that could be in any position to help, but nothing changed. My parents couldn't imagine that some of the things that were to bring me happiness were to become only memories. I was still a little boy and knew nothing about God's will prevailing in the lives of anyone He chooses.

Years of emotional turmoil followed, as they woke up every single day expecting the miracle they hoped for. Surely, they thought, it would only be a matter of time. But time stood still; year after year passed, and nothing happened.

If I could look back on my own life to see God's fingerprints in the small town, Okorase, I could now make sense of everything that seemed like a misfortune and a blemish on my life. It had taken many years before I understood how the Almighty God's hand in my life had shaped every event that came my way.

Through all the years when my situation became too overwhelming to embrace, I had to wonder why anything like this could happen to me. Why me? I can see how God molded my being in His hands and restored my hope even when my situation didn't seem to offer much hope. In hindsight, I have found how God was setting up the stage to transform me into a testimony of His own glory. But the shock in the moment and uncertainty of my future was painful to live through as a young boy. It must have been incredibly difficult for my parents to bear.

Perhaps they found some reassurance in the fact that all of us are indeed nothing more than clay in the Potter's hands. That is one image that has had a significant impact on my life and given me hope and the needed assurance that as long as my life is in God's hands, He will definitely make something good out of me.

Like the potter who sets out to transform a lump of clay into something desirable and beautiful to his own glory, the water to smooth the hard clay and the heat to harden the finished vessel, all works together as the potter intends. The unsuspecting clay ends up on a wheel to start the molding process, never knowing what it will become on the other side of the journey.

So when disappointment stared at me, I had a family who perhaps had to quietly tell themselves that "The Potter is still at work in our child's life." They had to believe it for themselves, and for me too. I was a young child then, but the discomfort piled on even more despondency as I grew into my adolescent years. Like a potter spending hours tirelessly working at a wheel to turn clay into something for the world to see, I was to spend the rest of my life with the understanding that Almighty God would shape my every step as seemed best to him.

Around the world, I can imagine there are many more people like you and me whose physical or emotional disabilities have altered the path they envisioned for themselves. The person will have to find a way to believe in their hearts, that whether or not someone can see, does not change the fact that you and I are still in His hands. We are. It may feel as though the creator of Heaven and Earth has left us to struggle through life on our own. I felt that way until I discovered the amazing truth that there is no moment that we are out of God's hands. I spent every waking day wondering when my fortunes would change.

Looking ahead was to be a challenge. Yet, as long as we can remind ourselves of this truth, whenever we come to a bridge of life that is so overwhelming due to something that either we or our society have made us believe, we can also proclaim that, "The Potter has not finished with us yet."

There once was a Bible story of the man Jeremiah, one of the most inspirational prophets who walked the face of this earth. Jeremiah was once at a very low point in his ministry. His nation had rebelled against God and heeded the counsel of false prophets who had led them to worship idols instead of Yahweh.

The Prophet Jeremiah was faced with the task of preaching repentance to a rebellious and backslidden nation. It was a difficult situation, but he understood this principle, that even in spite of the attitudes of a people who were bent on going as far as they could from God, they too were on the creator's worktable, and they too had a hope for their stories to bring God glory.

God was still determined to take what seemed to be an unyielding and rebellious life and turn it into something worthwhile and useful. Like the men and women in those days, I had to come to a point in my life where I could appreciate the fact that I was still on the spinning wheel of God. He loved me too much to allow what happened to me in that hospital room to become a wasted experience.

One of the most challenging encounters of my young life had to be when I came face to face with the truth that life was indeed a remarkable process in the hands of Almighty God, and would receive its perfection when God's light took center stage. Our part is to give the master craftsman enough room in our hearts to fashion us as seems best to Him.

In the face of what felt like a proverbial broken vessel, Jeremiah imagined how the potter never cast away the vessel that was not as he would want it—he made it over again. God can take anything—and anyone—and make them into something worthwhile and useful. The powerful part of that lesson is that what is perfect to you and me, is not what is perfect in God's eyes. What our society deems perfect, and whom our cultures define as worthy aren't the standard with which Almighty God sees you and me.

Even in our frailty, young or old, sick or well, God uses our journey and testimony for His glory. The blind, the deaf and the physically challenged are all in His perfect will and in His hands. The onlooker can stand back and admire the pot spinning on the potter's wheel as it turns into something beautiful until he presses it down again into what seems to us a mash of clay. If you and I were to ask the potter why he would do that, he might tell us that he was not finished with his work.

When I first read the Bible story of a man named Mephibosheth, there were so many incredible messages that stood out. The young man had been the son of another prominent royal, Jonathan and grandson of Israel's King Saul, and was born into a life of royalty, one where he wanted for nothing. His father and grandfather were the most prominent men in the whole nation, and it was as if his destiny was carved in stone to be one of happiness. Life soon turned to be very unfair for a young boy who was dealt with a hurdle he didn't choose.

Mephibosheth's life took a turn when at age five, his father died in battle against a Philistine army, and his grandfather soon after, took his own life to avoid being captured as a trophy. Suddenly, a young boy whose destiny was to probably inherit a place in his society was unsure of what would become of his fate. Mephibosheth's future was unraveling at the seams, and he was still a young boy.

All of this was happening at a time in Israel's history when it was not unusual for the lineage of a defeated king to suffer death at the hands of the conqueror. The victorious army would fight to wipe out the entire family of their opponents in the hope to avoid a future battle by the descendants to reclaim the throne.

In Mephibosheth's case, the young lady who was his caregiver, in a desperate effort to flee the town for his safety, accidentally dropped young Mephibosheth onto the floor. Overnight, the boy who was once happily running around like every other boy, lost his mobility. Suddenly, the young boy's world turned upside down. Perhaps through the years, the caregivers had done the best they could to take care of the little boy. Maybe one after the other, year after year, they had to leave him alone to find work elsewhere, and move on with their lives. Mephibosheth could not move on. He spent the rest of his life as a person with disability and was crushed. For his life, everything that had once been full of promise and privilege wiped away seemingly in an instant.

It was years later that King David found Mephibosheth in a town called Lo Debar and began a process of restoring him–physically and emotionally. He was to eat with the king every day, a great change from his life in filth and misery in Lo Debar. One of the intriguing dialogues between the two men happened when Mephibosheth asked King David why he would "notice a dead dog like me?"

He couldn't imagine any reason why the king David would even find it worth his time to invite him to sit and eat with him. That was how Mephibosheth saw himself–not even as a dog, but as a dead dog. He saw himself as worthless. If only Mephibosheth had a chance to see himself in the Potter's hand, then maybe he would have imagined a day that God would use his story to teach the world a lesson He couldn't have done any other way.

King David understood this simple truth about all of our human-ness. Even though he might not get Mephibosheth to walk or run again, there was a life full of hope and with an incredible testimony locked inside of Mephibosheth, so God could reach him even at his lowest point. Mephibosheth's physical disability had nurtured years of low self-worth. Perhaps at every dinner table, Mephibosheth would be reminded that he was not a dead dog. It could take days, months or even years, but someday Mephibosheth would have to accept deep in his heart that he too was worthy.

All of God's children are worthy. Our journeys may be completely different from each other, yet each and every one of us has been created in God's magnificent image, and that alone makes us worthy.

Our backgrounds have not been an accident. What may have happened to us, even as unbearable as it may have seemed, did not override the promise that Almighty God birthed into each of our hearts. Despite the misfortunes that other people have caused us, there is a Master Potter who is not finished with you and me and is working to bring us to a perfect end.

Regardless of which village or town or country a young child grows up in, our lives remain in the hands of Almighty God. Nothing about our lives is too trivial to His watchful eye. Even as we run through the days unaware of what lurks behind the next minute or the next turn, He alone knows what is best for us. Even when it looks like a dark cloud has taken over the rest of our lives, there is a God who is completely capable of raising the best of you and me out of what society has deemed to be worthless ashes, and of no value.

There could be a child somewhere who spent his early years doing everything a normal child would do, and suddenly his bones do not grow properly. Some conditions baffle the best doctors of the world, but nothing puzzles God. There could be persons who live their lives just as anyone would, only to find out one day that a debilitating disease leaves them in a wheelchair. Neither of these circumstances ought to signal the end of their world. Sure, it may turn out to become the most difficult chapter in a person's life, but certainly not the end.

I look back at my own life and am incredibly thankful to my parents and family who did not write me off when they couldn't understand why my childhood was smitten by a life-altering condition. I cannot thank enough the people with whom I have crossed paths, who did not allow me to give up on what my future could become. I have to be grateful they cared enough to remind me over and again that my life was carefully guarded in a Potter's hand.

Looking back, I cannot remember every thought that ran through my mind day and night, but I remember having to reset my focus on Almighty God, who is capable of using anyone's life, even my own, as a testimony.

Somehow, my parents had to convince themselves that no matter the uncertain ridges and valleys that would lie in their journey ahead, I was worth all their love and care. I was worth every kind of love because the God who created the universe and in whose hands I lay called me worthy. I was worth their affection, just like any of their other children. I was no different, and all through their struggle to find a doctor or clinic who would give them a different report about my life, I never left the potter's hands or His wheel.

It was to be many years before I embraced the truth that I was merely clay, and my Heavenly Father was determined to use my life however He saw fit. I have come to learn that the true turning points in anyone's life are the moments when, even while we think ourselves deficient, we lift our eyes and trust that God can still let His glory be manifested through us. A person's inability to use his/her legs or limbs effectively because of paralysis or pain doesn't change the destiny God has in store for him/her.

God does His greatest work in us at the most unexpected moments. Like a plant that grows every moment and every second, it is impossible to see this process by standing back and watching every bend and shake. The challenge for you and me is to give our very best to the people God has placed in our lives and in our societies, even when it looks like a lost cause. The amazing fact is that in the eyes of our Heavenly Father, no cause is lost.

All of us are indeed worth His love, and worth His grace. We are indeed worthy.

CHAPTER 2

THE MUD

God's Way, not Our Own

As he said this, he spat on the ground and made clay of the spittle and anointed the man's eyes with the clay. John 9:6

I did not see the oncoming train. The last moment I could remember was when my car was spinning after a forceful impact along the railroad tracks.

It was an early morning in April. I had left home with my wife and children on our way to drop them off at school. I had decided this morning to find an alternative route to the school so they would arrive on time.

We were to drive through Abelemkpe, a suburb of the capital city, Accra. From there, I would drive across the railroad tracks into the next town, Alajo. The tracks seldom had any trains on them; hence that intersection was hardly a busy one and scarcely demanded any attention at all. Occasionally when a train passed, anyone standing nearby could see it coming from several kilometers in the distance, and get a safe distance away until it passed. But this particular morning was one of the very few days I encountered an oncoming train.

Soon after I had crossed the railroad tracks, my car, a Ford Escape sports utility vehicle, got stuck in the mud. There was nothing unusual about this. Plus, there were often many young people in the area that you could call for help. This time was different.

It had rained heavily the previous night. The area was quiet and deserted. I was unaware the road was damaged, especially around the railroad tracks. There were no warning signs anywhere, and no one nearby.

A train suddenly appeared in the distance. For a moment, it felt like a dream or a scary movie. I thought perhaps all I had to do was blink and it would be gone. What seemed like an ordinary moment suddenly turned into a case of life and death. Tragedy had come knocking at our doorstep, and all we had was a few seconds to scramble our way out of the mud.

My heart began to race. The train was approaching at full speed. Every inch of my body was shaking as I hurried to get myself and family to safety. We had to get off the tracks. But we were stuck in the mud.

I pressed the car's accelerator as hard as I could. I knew that the front of the car was already over the railroad tracks, but the back half was still trapped on the tracks. We were terrified. Nothing I did to my car seemed to work. I knew if I tried to get out and pull my children out of the car seat, all of us would be in much more harm as we might not get out of the way in time.

The best option was to press on and get the whole car off the tracks. I was stuck in mud, and my children were tucked in the backseat unsure of what to do. I applied full acceleration, but no matter how fast the tires spun in the mud, the car would not budge. I decided to reverse quickly, but that didn't work either. My wife and my eldest child made separate attempts to open the doors and run, but the doors automatically shut and none of their last-ditch efforts worked.

It was too late to do anything else, and this was happening so fast. That could have been our last moment alive. But God had other plans.

The train ran into our car at full speed and with such incredible force that for a split moment we couldn't fully comprehend what was happening. The train rammed into the side and crushed the fuel tank into the trunk. The vehicle spun around, and our faces smashed into the airbags from the dashboard, steering wheel, and doors.

Out of nowhere, a group of young men rushed onto the scene and pulled my family out of the car to safety. We sat on the ground, terrified and breathing frantically. My wife and children were not harmed, but visibly shaken after such a close call. My mind raced. Where did this train suddenly appear from and where was it heading? Why couldn't it have been any other day? And I wondered where all the people had been just a few moments earlier. It was as if God has a strange lesson for us to learn, and he would have no one nearby to interrupt it.

We had survived. We sat on the ground, at a loss for words.

Government officials soon came to inspect the damage. They determined that the car was a wreck, and asked how we were doing. We had been stuck in the car together, but when the dust settled, we had walked away unscathed. It was nothing short of a miracle. I cannot fully comprehend what my wife and children must have gone through in those final moments as the train slammed into our car, but I am confident that it had been the saving grace of God that kept us all safe.

A few hours later, we were discharged from the Police Hospital in Cantonments; none of us had sustained any injuries. Indeed, the hand of the Lord had delivered us from the claws of death. I was almost speechless, having experienced the saving power of Christ that fateful morning. I pondered what a powerful symbol the accident had been.

The mud had been a figurative and literal bumpy situation for us and hindered us from going forward, but God was soon to use that for His own glory. When I had done everything I knew how to do, it was left to Jesus' protective hand to ensure that we would live again. In that desperate moment, we could only scream a prayer. Nothing else mattered.

If indeed the devil had meant for that moment to be the end of our lives, God had created a way of escape for us. God was saying to us that he had much more for us to accomplish and that we were to share His message of hope even when the situation had seemed so hopeless that we couldn't find our way out on our own.

Often, when I think about the symbolism of the mud, I think of the kind of scenario where we are trapped and unable to move ahead. There are many men and women whose lives make them feel stuck in mud for years. Whatever burdens we have been forced to live with, the God who sets our days and knows every second of our lives knows exactly what He will do to make our way of escape, and our testimony is redirected to glorify His name.

The Bible tells a story of an extraordinary miracle Jesus performed.

> *¹ As he went along, he saw a man blind from birth.*
> *² His disciples asked him, "Rabbi, who sinned, this man or his parents, that he was born blind?"*
> *³ "Neither this man nor his parents sinned," said Jesus, "but this happened so that the works of God might be displayed in him.*
> *⁴ As long as it is day, we must do the works of him who sent me. Night is coming, when no one can work.*
> *⁵ While I am in the world, I am the light of the world."*
> *⁶ After saying this, he spit on the ground, made some mud with the saliva, and put it on the man's eyes. ⁷ "Go," he told him, "wash in the Pool of Siloam" (this word means "Sent"). So the man went and washed, and came home seeing.*
>
> John 9:1-6 (NIV)

Chapter 2: The Mud

The mud should not hold us back.

It is remarkable to discover that you and I could be stuck in the same circumstance or mind frame for so long that we can come to accept it as our portion in life. The mud Jesus put on the man's eyes, though surely uncomfortable, did not get stuck on him forever; rather, it began the healing process, and he came back after washing in the Pool of Siloam, seeing. Whether or not a situation changes in the physical realm doesn't mean that Christ's grace is insufficient for our lives.

So Jesus healed the man, with mud. Unusual, but it was as if mud was supposed to be a metaphor for our own lives, like blinding obstacles that soon dry into small chips of clay and sand that peel away.

The miracle ahead of us may not be one we anticipate, or happen in a way we expect. The miracle can be in God's transformative power to use any hindrance or supposed shortcoming to bring Him glory. He alone can use any insignificant moment to change a life forever.

Jesus was to perform a miracle that would become a testimony to many across the Jewish land, and to the ends of the world, and in His infinite wisdom, He chose mud to accomplish this. Almighty God could have just healed the blind man even without touching his eyes. He did not have to touch him. He didn't even have to speak to him. He didn't have to spit in the sand to turn it into the mud. He did not need the mud to rub on the man's eyes for him to wash off. What I am confident about is that God did not need the water in any pool to heal the blind man. Yet that is precisely what He did.

The resurrection power of Jesus Christ could and can raise anything from death to life. There is no physical or emotional situation or challenge that God cannot change in one instant. Morever, there is no mental disability or any affliction so troubling that the grace of God cannot heal it. But He alone chooses when, and precisely how He does anything. When Jesus met the man born blind whose story would be told for many generations to come, God chose the mud. He chose the dust.

One thing I learned many years ago was the simple truth that no matter how we crave to know the will and the heart of God, in our humanity, our ways will never be God's ways. We may never understand His ways. Ultimately, He alone is God, and He chooses when to rub mud in the eyes of a man born blind. He alone can do what seems unusual to us, but ultimately the fact that it brings Him the glory is what is most important.

God restores. He is still in the business of making diamonds out of dust in us. He is still in the business of taking the people whom society shuns, because they do not measure up to some standard, and using them for His glory.

Jesus, in choosing to heal the man born blind the way he did, saw eyebrows raised, especially in the religious sections of the community. Maybe their discontent would have been less if Jesus had chosen another day to heal the man born blind. Even more, maybe they would have seen it as totally understandable if Jesus had given the man a good reason why that time was not the best time for the miracle. Jesus chose the moment in which he found the man as the best moment, and he chose mud. Why? Because he could. The same God who took dust and breathed into it to form man, could at any time take the same dust and use it to perform a miracle that would confound the religious leaders and everyone who had seen Jesus all his life and didn't think much of him.

The disciples discovered the truth about the cause of the man's blindness—the God factor. By this, Jesus shifted his disciples' attention from sin to God, whose works needed to be manifested in the man. This was not the first time Jesus was referring to the works of his Father. In much the same way, on healing the paralytic on the Sabbath, Jesus told the Jews that "My father is working still and I am working."

John 5:17.

The implication of this statement is that there was no break in the Father's work even on the Sabbath, and Jesus, who manifested the Father's work, needed to emulate him.

Jesus drew their attention to the works of God and how they needed to be fulfilled. This obligation for Jesus and his disciples was time-bound–they were supposed to perform the works "while it is day." Was he talking in literal terms or figuratively? Was he referring to the normal 6 a.m.–6 p.m. daytime or a specific period marked as "day"? From all indications, it could be deduced that they were to make good use of the opportune time at their disposal. Therefore, the reference should not be taken literally to mean regular daytime.

Theologians through the years have asserted that the "day" referred to the historical presence of Jesus and his ongoing ministry by means of which he accomplished the works of the Father. The coming of the "night" was going to bring every work to a standstill, for at night, no one could work, or work effectively. It was therefore incumbent on Jesus and his disciples to work tirelessly during the "day" to make the passage of the "night" a mere formality.

Like the day, the night had also been used figuratively and may represent a time when Jesus was to be absent from the human story. The "night" therefore was going to be a period where the opportunities of doing the works of God were going to be curtailed, hence Jesus' admonition to do the works of the one who had sent him while it was day.

For you and me, the "day" may very well represent the opportunities for us and the people whose paths cross with ours. The "night" may be the moments when we look back and find the opportunities that we have missed to uplift someone.

All of us, regardless of our status in society, are not exempt from the call to seek to make a difference in the lives of people whenever we can. There are hundreds and thousands of persons with disability roaming our streets every day, many of whom have resigned themselves to society's view that they are burdens and have nothing to contribute. Even for them, God is counting on you and me to use the "mud" in the moment where we stand to touch the proverbial eyes.

A few years ago, in September, I was scheduled for an examination, the first of such computerized exams I would take in my adult life. The striking difference would be that the result would be displayed immediately on the monitor at the end of the thirty-minute duration. That was just as nerve-wracking as it was stirring. The exam was to be thirty objective questions, and I needed to answer twenty-one correctly in order to pass. When I keyed in the code I had been given, the clock started ticking, and I had to hurry up and finish on time.

A challenge I had grappled with much of my life was finishing any exam on time. This time, I was bent on answering all the questions and answering them correctly. The pressure was intense because the life of my entire family could change based on the outcome. My failure would be a big blow to the family, and I was determined to move every mountain to excel. The exam started. I answered most of the questions as best as I could, and those I did not know I would skip and proceed to the next question. My plan was to later come back to make sure I had answered every one of them to the best of my knowledge. I did not leave any question unanswered, and this time I finished on time.

I clicked the button, and the result displayed immediately. It was a huge sigh of relief to find that I had passed. I was happily sitting patiently waiting for the supervisor. When she saw my results, she seemed pretty surprised, exclaiming, "Oouuuuuwh, you have passed!"

I thought to myself, "Of course, I did." I hadn't gone into the room expecting to fail, but the supervisor was visibly shocked that I had a passing score. It was not hard to see that she was not expecting anything more than failure from me, so she was stunned to see my success.

The exam was a test to obtain a driver's license. In any other case it wouldn't be anything odd, but for the supervisor, just my being in the room alone was somewhat baffling. Ghana's Driver and Vehicle Licensing Authority (DVLA) probably did not have many persons with disabilities roaming their hallways for their turn to take a driver's exam. My family had something to celebrate because they now had a driver with a valid license, who would take them to school, and run errands for them. As routine as these seem, this was something I couldn't have done for many years, but in its own time that happened.

It was also a challenging time in my ministry, because I was aware that I would be posted to a congregation that had no accommodation or duty car for the minister. This meant that I had to go and make my own transportation arrangements. This may seem quite unusual to many, but it happened. I needed to find a strategy that would make us survive the hustle and tussle of city life. Earlier on, I had imported a disability-friendly car from Canada, and that was why I needed a driver's license.

In my own world, I walked out of those hallways feeling like the man born blind whose eyes Jesus had rubbed with mud for him to see again. The world of possibilities was opened because my travel opportunities would no longer be at the mercy of others who would have to sacrifice their time and effort to help me get where I needed to go.

Jesus spat on the ground, made mud with the saliva and spread it on the man's eyes to begin the healing process. I am thankful to have Jesus' as a loving father whose ways are much higher than my own, and who can choose to use spit as a healing agent.

I remember the first time I came across the three components of healing miracles: healing power, healing touch, and healing agent. There was power transmission from Jesus to the man though it was not immediately seen; Jesus touched him as He anointed his eyes with clay, and the spittle and water from the pool of Siloam were the healing agents.

The most striking lesson in this example to me became the fact that Jesus chooses how to heal and when to heal. In the earlier chapters of the same Gospel of John, the Bible records another incredible miracle of

Jesus reaching out to bring hope to a man whose life had been sidelined for many years.

> ² *Now there is in Jerusalem near the Sheep Gate a pool, which in Aramaic is called Bethesda[a] and which is surrounded by five covered colonnades.*
> ³ *Here a great number of disabled people used to lie—the blind, the lame, the paralyzed.* [4] [b] ⁵ *One who was there had been an invalid for thirty-eight years.*
> ⁶ *When Jesus saw him lying there and learned that he had been in this condition for a long time, he asked him, "Do you want to get well?"*
> ⁷ *"Sir," the man replied, "I have no one to help me into the pool when the water is stirred. While I am trying to get in, someone else goes down ahead of me."*
> ⁸ *Then Jesus said to him, "Get up! Pick up your mat and walk."*
> ⁹ *At once the man was cured; he picked up his mat and walked.*
>
> John 5:2-9 (NIV)

What I found intriguing was how Jesus took the time to inquire about the man's state of mind, and indeed his heart. Was the man willing to allow the saving grace of Jesus to restore his heart to move towards his potential, or would he instead rest at the same place and wallow in the same self-pity for another 38 years?

But when Jesus met the man who had been born blind at the Pool of Siloam, he never engaged in any form of conversation before he applied the mud to his eyes. Jesus must have known his heart. He did not seek his consent before he took this action.

Researchers have argued that, in that society "spittle was believed to be of a medicinal value" and that the use of spittle was generally accompanied by magical feats. There was the perception that Judaism abhorred the practice of using saliva and charm to heal a wound. In Jesus' case, he did not spit on the man, but rather on the ground, and his action was also not accompanied by any magical words or practices. It is easy to recognize how spitting in this context was different from the manner in which it is used in exorcisms and other magic acts of that era. But did Jesus have to use mud at all?

As we travel through our quiet days I hope we all get to experience the fact that Jesus still uses things that seem worthless to you and me to change ordinary moments into extraordinary encounters. Where his grace abounds, a life stuck in mud is renewed; a life without sight sees again.

Did I have to be stuck in mud and come face to face with death for my testimony to be worth sharing?

Of course not!

But He, Almighty God, chose the mud.

CHAPTER 3

A GLIMPSE OF AMAZING GRACE

The Invisible Disabilities in our Own Lives

¹ As he passed by, he saw a man blind from his birth.
² And his disciples asked him, "Rabbi, who sinned, this man,
or his parents that he was born blind"? John 9:1, 2.

What will a little boy do when he cannot see the sun's rays and the beautiful birds that roam the skies, like you and me? What is that young man to do when all he can do is smell the fresh flowers along the fields where he walks, but everything in the world around him is the same? What if a person cannot see or hear is not the only window to the world because the community around him or her will make all the difference?

What about the woman whose hurdle we cannot see? Her heart hurts every time she lives through the world that seems to have forgotten all about her. People see her, and accept her for what they see, but will never know the brokenness that she cannot find the words to describe.

What will that little girl's dream become, when her family finds no value in how she has come to this world, and rejects her even before she can find a warm hand to touch? What happened to the young man, who had once run through the woods and swum in the gentle rivers, when somehow, unfortunately, his life took a different turn — his legs no longer help him walk — and none of what he could once do so easily, is possible anymore?

There is a remarkable truth about the life we live, one that points to the fact that irrespective of who we are and what we have come to believe about ourselves, none of us will walk through life without our own handicaps. We all admit that we are not perfect by any means, but we do not wake up in the morning and look at ourselves in the mirror to imagine how unworthy we are. We see the best in ourselves, and thank our Creator for whatever He has given to us, and however He has made us. Our inability to perform a task or live a fulfilling life as we probably could, does not define us. We accept our hurdles, but reassure ourselves that we are prized jewels, at least in one person's eyes, even if those eyes are our own.

Yet we do not mind if another person's inability to run as fast as he could have, hear as clearly as he could have, or see as far as he could, defines him. The reality is that, no matter how cleverly we rewrite it, nothing will change the fact that all of us have some form of constraint. Our own shortcomings or disabilities, in whatever form they may take, are something only God's grace can use for His own glory.

When other people and society define what they see as our flaws, they will assign their own meaning to them, and describe them as a void in our lives. Sure, they could give any condition a name they find appropriate, but who is to say what part of our abilities or inabilities Almighty God needs for His own glory?

I have found over and again that what we pay attention to most often — and perhaps as a function of our humanness — is what we see. So we see others' inadequacy, not our own. Because we cannot imagine ourselves as having any shortcoming, we can conveniently hide behind the cloak of community to ignore the pain of our brother or sister who lives with one challenge or another.

So it could be that even where there exists a challenge, if it doesn't make its way to the surface of our lives for everyone to be able to point to, we convince ourselves it doesn't exist. Other times, we conveniently push it farther and farther away, rather than accepting that no matter who we are, we are created in the image of Almighty God and wonderfully made. We see the seeming imperfections in every other person's life, rather than seeing for a moment that they too have been wonderfully made by Almighty God.

Toiling underneath the daily grind that we call our life, we are often too busy to see the empty spaces in that life. I learned very early in life that none of our lives are perfect, but it is only through the saving grace of Jesus Christ's salvation that we are made whole, and this truth transcends physical or mental disability. Without grace, none of us could be worthy.

I remember the enthusiasm that drove me to the doorstep of Trinity Theological Seminary, in Legon, Ghana. I was embarking on a dream and a calling to be trained as a minister of the Presbyterian Church of Ghana. This passion was dulled almost immediately when I crossed paths with a young man whom I had known for many years, Jefferson. He had recently become a minister and had come back to the seminary for further studies. I was thrilled to be at the seminary and I wore the joy on my face.

Jefferson couldn't hide his thoughts, "Didn't the church authorities see you before you were admitted?" he quizzed me.

For a moment, I hoped I had not heard him say those words. I was quiet and did not have the words to respond. Sadly, I knew what my friend meant. I had a physical disability, and in his mind, he couldn't imagine who, knowing how society frowned on disability, will admit me to the institution. Sadly, he wouldn't be the only person who shared those sentiments, and I wondered how the rest of my life at Trinity would unfold if those were the first words of my own friend.

The rest of the night was one of the most difficult of my life. I kept asking myself, "Do I belong here?" "Have I made a wrong choice by availing myself to be trained as a minister of the church?" The flurry of questions continued. "What have I done wrong that I should outwit the church authorities before coming to the seminary?" "Does the church frown on persons with disabilities?"

Here I was on the campus of a seminary where men and women from all walks of life trained to become ambassadors of Jesus Christ, and my first encounter was the farthest it could be from anything Christ-like. I knew my friend was referring to my disability, and his facial expressions said everything his words had failed to say. To him, it was incomprehensible to see me becoming a minister of the church. From that day on, I began a solemn reflection on disability and the theological concerns associated with it.

What I didn't have the words to tell Jefferson was that though we all have the perfect image of God, we had all come to the school with a myriad of imperfections, for however nice one's body looks, it is corruptible. None of us by nature was perfect; it is only in Christ Jesus that our imperfections are absolved, and we receive imputed righteousness. But the world could fail to see all of humanity as being created in the perfect image of the Almighty God; Christians cannot miss that truth.

Unfortunately, this is the worldview of society that has found its way into the Church, so much that gradually our outlook is no longer much different from that of an unbeliever, whose guide isn't the same amazing grace that turns you and me, wretched sinners, into children of the Almighty God.

I entered the seminary with an undergraduate degree in Religious Studies. This background, and some academic exemptions, qualified me to join a class that had begun a year ahead of me. Coincidentally, I was sitting in the same lecture hall with my friend Jefferson, and we ended up doing most of the courses together. With his comments tucked away, I related very well to him and he eventually became my study partner. We were also praying together. We got closer as friends and spent much of the time talking about our lives beyond academic work.

Soon I learned one unexpected fact about Jefferson. He also had a disability, an intellectual one. Jefferson could not concentrate for more than a few moments at a time, so the long stretches of vigorous academic work were a challenge for him. His condition often got worse, especially in the afternoons, to such an extent that anytime he tried, he would get a severe headache and would leave his studies to go and have a rest.

In the evenings, he would come to my room, for me to take him through everything that had transpired in the lecture hall that day. Through our discussions, he was able to understand the topics, and that was enough for him. It was this approach that helped him to complete the program. My condition had changed, and maybe if Jefferson ever remembered his own words, he would have to wonder how the same person, whose admission to the seminary had posed a problem to him (Jefferson) initially, had now become instrumental to his success.

Jefferson emerged as a first-class student, and I also earned first-class recognition. During all our time as students, however, only a few people knew Jefferson's problem. No one saw his disability. Even Jefferson himself had never seen his own problem as a disability. It was not a disability in his eyes, because society didn't see it as such. Jefferson, like most of us, saw everyone's imperfections except his own.

He was quick to see my disability, just because it was obvious, for I walked with the help of a stick. Jefferson had a hidden disability. During the periods I was taking him through his studies, I could have asked him the same question he asked me on my first day at the seminary, "Didn't the church authorities see you before you were admitted?" I could imagine what his answer would have been. Though I had a disability, it was not a blind spot in my life. I have come to accept my difficulties and have done my best to live with them. My reality was no longer a blind spot because it had come under the spotlight of God.

In much the same way, I encourage each and every one of us to unveil his/her disabilities, weaknesses, and shortfalls in order to come under the merciful spotlight of God and receive His attention. Most of us, just as in the case of my friend Jefferson, have "hidden disabilities," but are quick to see the "disabilities" of others. We are quick to wonder what may have caused the challenge or the disability.

What we do not know or understand, we assign our own meanings to, and we believe the stories we tell ourselves. The last thing we often employ is empathy and grace, with nothing in our being allowing us to imagine, what if the tables were turned and it was us in that predicament? Our society does a remarkable job of labelling the disabilities around us, especially when they are obvious.

That reality is no different in many cultures across the globe, where it is often accepted, even implicitly, to equate disability with sin. In many minds, someone's sin or mistake must have caused the disability. Sadly as it turns out, it is easy for anyone to cast off another person whose condition we cannot fully understand, rather than taking a moment to express genuine empathy.

One thing my friend Jefferson had not fully come to terms with is the fact that Almighty God in His own wisdom often chooses the perceived weak people in a crowd and gives them the strength to fully depend on Him. God uses the situations that seem improbable to do the impossible so that His glory will be manifested through the lives that He touches.

In 1 Corinthians 1: 25-29, the apostle Paul writes,

> "*25 For the foolishness of God is wiser than human wisdom, and the weakness of God is stronger than human strength.*

> *²⁶ Brothers and sisters, think of what you were when you were called. Not many of you were wise by human standards; not many were influential; not many were of noble birth.*
> *²⁷ But God chose the foolish things of the world to shame the wise; God chose the weak things of the world to shame the strong.*
> *²⁸ God chose the lowly things of this world and the despised things—and the things that are not—to nullify the things that are,*
> *²⁹ so that no one may boast before him."*

The reassuring truth is that God, who created the universe and every living being that walks the face of the earth, sees beyond our physical, mental and emotional disabilities. Whether we are blind or hard of hearing, God's hand has fearfully and masterfully created each and every one of us, and intentionally breathed life into us. Nothing about any of us is an accident. Nothing in our lives that we endure is a surprise to God, not even our disabilities.

Through the years, I recall stories in the Bible where God called the prophet Isaiah, a man with a glowing reputation for doing God's work, but who still saw himself as unworthy. In his own eyes, Isaiah could not help but see himself as "a man of unclean lips and [who] dwelt among a people of unclean lips," Isaiah 6:5.

The prophet Jeremiah was no different. He also gave the excuse that he did not know how to speak, for he was only a child. Another remarkable character, Moses, had a speech disability, and he wanted God to consider that before He thought of sending him to orchestrate one of the most remarkable rescue missions in history. But in all these instances, God insisted on sending the people He had chosen on the assignments for which He had called them.

Even more intriguing, God had no intention of using their respective "disabilities" to exclude them. Indeed, He chooses what seems to you and me as the "foolish things" and "unworthy" people and sets them on extraordinary missions. Maybe this was at the heart of the apostle Paul's writing when he described the "disability" in his life as "thorns in his flesh." I cannot imagine for a moment that he lived with this pain and challenge with a happy heart every day.

I can imagine he must have gone through years where he imagined what value would come of his disability, and if he wouldn't be helping the kingdom much more if that disability were peeled away from his life.

I found many years ago that every one of us is yearning to close the chapter on our own "disability." We would do almost anything to pretend our lives are devoid of flaws. It is even more unfortunate when the disability is the kind we can conveniently conceal, rather than allowing God's all-sufficient grace to carry us through it. In our weaknesses, we lean on the grace of God. In our weaknesses, we can tap into God's power that makes us perfect. In our weaknesses, the beauty of God is revealed in us.

If there is one striking argument against our living in denial, it would be that rather than denying our vulnerabilities in order to present ourselves as "world champions," we should be reminded of King Solomon's words in Ecclesiastes,

> *"I have seen something else under the sun: The race is not to the swift or the battle to the strong, nor does food come to the wise or wealth to the brilliant or favor to the learned; but time and chance happen to them all."*
>
> Ecclesiastes 9:11.

One's swiftness, strength, wisdom, brilliance, and education cannot — and will not — automatically put him ahead of the disadvantaged in society, for "time and chance happen to them all."

I was about twenty-six by the time I enrolled at the S.D.A. Teacher Training College, in Asokore-Koforidua, in Ghana's Eastern Region. The unusual turn of events happened to me when I climbed up the stage to be recognized at the school's annual Speech and Prize Giving Day. That was an event that recognized students who had been exemplary in a field of study or extracurricular activity. I won the best Physical Education Student prize, and that was to the surprise of many of the people who had gathered in the auditorium that afternoon.

It was unfathomable to see a student with an obvious disability winning that prize in an arena that you would imagine would be reserved for the strongest student, the fastest runner, or the most gifted athlete. I was probably standing on the stage at the expense of the other students whom society would imagine as the "swift" and the "strong."

I later learned that the college bursar who sat next to the Physical Education tutor's husband curiously asked, "What event does he do?" This question must have been on the minds of many on that day. What they didn't know was that in the first year at the college, all that we did in Physical Education class was theory. We did not set foot on any field; neither did the course require us to take even one step.

The playing field was a neutral one, and interestingly the other students who were so eager to display their athletic prowess never cared to apply themselves in the theory section. I made sure I left no stone unturned, to make a mark in this area of study.

Many persons with disabilities are doing their best to satisfy themselves with and pursue their goals and aspirations in life, and nobody should discourage them or put an impediment in their way. We must all, as humans, develop that attitude, to help break the barrier that limits and inhibits our participation.

Because the things we see with our eyes become the basis of how we interpret the world around us, we miss the chance to see the whole picture, which includes the blind spots in our own lives. For persons born blind, their white canes lead them everywhere they go. Through the streets and among the crowds, they have no way to hide their disability. But there is nothing in this world that suggests that the person's white cane is a badge of inadequacy, or a sign of anything more than just a man whose journey is colored slightly differently from our own.

It is the same for the person whose inability to walk effortlessly while everyone seems to be passing, busily travelling through their day. We see the hurdles they have to live with. We can only imagine what goes through their minds and hearts when we run past them, but they have to take all the time they can just for the next step.

There are many people whose disability leaves them sitting in one place and unable to move on their own. Their shortcomings are glaring. We see them. For some of these men and women, we share in their disability; for others we show concern. For most, however, the feeling is apathy. We do not stop for a moment to care. We do not care enough to think genuinely. We do not think long and hard enough to act. It is their story, not ours. Society finds a nice way to shrug off the challenge and the discomfort in someone else's journey, and turn a blind eye to it.

The blind spot — just as in every area of life — becomes the point of our own lives: that our view is so obstructed that we cannot see what otherwise is so obvious. Maybe if we saw the spots clearly as the next person, we would do all we could to change them. In many areas of our own lives, there can be things we may have hoped would be different. Even though we all have shortcomings, because not all shortcomings are visible, it is easy to walk through life and live in a bubble.

One of the most amazing things in life is the fact that everyone has a story, and each is incredibly unique. It is impossible to know everyone's story unless he/she opens up to share it. Because of this truth, it is much easier to ignore the person who stands or sits next to us. We do not have any obligation to imagine where they have come from or what their journey may have looked like.

Our own blind spots shield us away from honestly pausing for a moment to share in someone else's pain, discomfort, challenge or journey. Maybe we are too busy. Maybe we have our own lives to worry ourselves over, and not enough time in a day to concern ourselves with another's.

As a pastor, I have worked with churches and para-church organizations across Ghana and some parts of Africa. Unfortunately, inside the Christian faith, we miss the chance to truly reflect Jesus to people who find their way into churches dejected and broken down. A Christian's vantage point in relating to others should not be predicated on what society instructs. The people with physical disabilities — what everyone can easily see — leave the churches still feeling like an afterthought in society.

As we go throughout our everyday life, like a person driving fast on a road, no matter how expensive or comfortable the car we drive in may be, there is only so much the car's mirrors reveal to us as we rush past it all. At any point, some events unfold right next to us, many of which we will never see, and it is that reality that should at least force us to pause and hear another person's heart. When we hear a person's heart, we will be more inclined to see them more for who they truly are, and be moved to act.

The beauty of life is not to walk through it wearing masks that conceal our true heart, our pain, and even our difficulty. Whatever obstacle another person lives with is not a measuring stick to define what their life could become.

It is never too late to challenge ourselves to rethink how we have trained our minds to perceive the challenge of the person standing next to us. They may be blind, or deaf. They may have spent their lives in a wheelchair, or having to rely on another person to help them through some of the ordinary events you and I go through every day. But the fact remains, that person — no matter where he is in life today — has gotten there by grace, bestowed on the children of God. He is indeed worthy.

CHAPTER

4

SRI LANKA

Understanding the Plight of People who Feel Alone

> *"We must work the works of him who sent me while it is day; night comes when no one can work."* John 9:4

The World Council of Churches held an international conference on "Theology of Diakonia for the 21st Century" in Colombo, the commercial capital and largest city of *Sri Lanka*. It had been slated for the first week of June 2012.

It was about a week before the conference, and I still did not know my fate, whether or not I would receive an invitation to participate. It had been over five months to that date, when Dr. Sam Kabue, the Programme Executive for the Ecumenical Disability Advocates Network (EDAN), sent an email to inform me to prepare to represent EDAN in the forthcoming conference. I waited for weeks and months, and it appeared that what seemed like an invitation to one of the most uplifting events in my ministry work would never come.

Then on 25 May 2012, I received a mail from Eggli Silvia who was working at the time as staff at the World Council of Churches office in Geneva, Switzerland. Silvia inquired whether I was still interested in attending the conference, and I imagined she was unsure if the short window of notification would give me ample time to prepare for my trip from Accra.

I still had to make travel arrangements, some of which I couldn't have done without the official invitation letter. She stressed, however, that the organizers would be glad to see me there. I agreed that despite the time constraint, I was going to do my best to attend. This meant that I and the organizers needed to double up in our efforts to make this a reality.

Five days later, I received the necessary documents, including the visa and the plane ticket to leave for Sri Lanka. I was looking forward to a successful conference, and truly grateful for the team members who were working around the clock to make it a memorable one.

I was on the same flight to *Bandaranaike* International Airport with Mrs. Gertrude Fefoame. Gertrude was a member of EDAN, who at the time, also resided in Ghana, and we had been collaborating in doing disability work, both across Ghana and in neighboring countries. Her presence on the flight and the trip was very assuring to me. At least I had found someone who would understand me and could easily share memories.

We left Accra on the last day of May 2012. We were scheduled for transit in Dubai, United Arab Emirates. But in Accra, I reported late for the check-in, and my saving grace was the fact that the flight had been delayed for well over thirty minutes. As I made my way onto the plane, I mumbled to myself quietly, with relief, that God probably had something special for me to find in Sri Lanka. That must have been why He had made it possible for me to attend the conference despite the hurdles that seemed to find a way to derail my plan at every turn.

This was my first trip outside Africa. One of the things that excited me on the flight was the map which showed the plane's trajectory as we crossed the Red Sea. It was particularly fascinating in its own way as I tried to imagine the Israelites' story in the Bible when God parted the Red Sea for their exodus from Egypt.

Here I was, flying over the Red Sea, and a small voice in my heart seemed to say, *"The problems I see today, I will never see again in my life; the battle is the Lord's, therefore, I should remain calm."* For the same God whose hand was guiding me into a world far from the one I had always known, would bring to fruition His purpose and intents capsulated in me. While the Israelites had gone through an underpass, I reasoned that mine was a flyover. But it was the same Red Sea. I chuckled at that thought.

Eight long hours and fifteen minutes later, we were in Dubai Airport. I waited for another hour and a half before we boarded another plane en route to Bandaranaike Airport, in Colombo. We arrived in the middle of the afternoon, where we were welcomed by our host, the National Christian Council of Sri Lanka. I calmly look around at the sights from the airport to Pegasus Reef Hotel, about 35 minutes' drive from Bandaranaike.

The Pegasus Reef Hotel stood right on the shores of the Indian Ocean, 200 metres away from the Helakandah Beach, and was a delightful choice for many tourists. It also brought into memory the worst tsunami the world had ever experienced.

The hotel had once been destroyed by the December 2004 tsunami, when the entire Sri Lankan island was severely hit by the storms, earthquake, and strong winds from the Indian Ocean. Adding to Sri Lanka's difficult past was the fact that the country had been at civil war for twenty-six years, with the Tamir Tigers fighting the government forces. The war, which had lasted from 1983 to 2009, had left devastating effects on the entire lives of the Sri Lankans.

At the time of the conference, the cost of the war was still being counted. Sri Lanka might have been carefully chosen for the conference, perhaps to give the participants an opportunity to reflect deeply and give responses to the problems that threatened human existence. If a country was dealing with a crushing crisis and a disability population, Sri Lanka could not have been left out, for the war had maimed quite a number of people. Maybe the inherent hope was that being in a place like this would urge us to embark on deliberations with lasting impact, that would affect more than just the participants of the conference.

In Sri Lanka, I found that Gertrude and I were the only persons with disabilities invited to the conference. So who were the rest of the participants? There were about fifty people from all walks of life and countries around the world, all carefully chosen to represent aspects their societies tried their best to overlook. There were participants whose expertise covered issues like homelessness, migrant workers, the Dalits of India, the Church in Palestine, the HIV/AIDS epidemic, and the plight of persons with disabilities. There were also representatives and displaced people from war-torn countries whose fate had become like that of Sri Lanka.

There were also some national church leaders attending, including the Anglican Bishop of Panama and the Methodist Bishop of Togo. The World Council of Churches had organized this conference to help look at how diakonia would be understood and appropriated in creative ways in different parts of the world. *Diakonia* is a popular Christian theological word that has its root in the Greek language, and which embraces a call to serve the poor and oppressed. The underlying passion is to meet the needs of the marginalized and vulnerable in society and take the grace and gifts of the Church to the world that desperately needs them.

On the last day of the conference, the EDAN team was given the opportunity to conduct the morning devotion. Gertrude (I called her Aunty Gerty) asked me to preach while she led the service. That morning, at breakfast time before the devotion, I sat at the table with Straussman. Straussman was also a participant from the one of the countries in the Americas . He was curious to know why I wore a clerical outfit. I explained to him that I was scheduled to preach at devotion that morning. Immediately, his countenance changed. He remained silent for some time. Judging from his expression, it was not difficult to read what was on Straussman's mind.

At the various plenary sessions, Straussman and I had lengthy discussions about the cancer of discrimination, the dangerous effects of stereotyping, and a host of challenges that led to the exclusion of the persons with disability by our communities.

Strangely, we were still at the conference and here was I, being looked down upon by a co-participant. If a participant who had flown several thousands of miles to Asia for this purpose, cannot rid himself of the prejudices and preconceived notions about a person with a disability, then who can? I never expected such behavior from Straussman, and I had assumed he would be happy to see me leading the devotion.

Finally, Straussman broke his silence.

"I am going to do two things for you; I am going to pray for you, and also expect something great from you," he said.

I knew he was being sarcastic. His attitude was incredibly unfortunate, but it was evident that the challenges of the people who live with disability are much deeper than an occasional stare and ridicule. Straussman's attitude reminded me of my friend Jefferson a few years earlier. Jefferson had been a colleague whom I had met on my first day at the seminary, and whose remark about why the institution accepted a person with my disability left me with an unfortunate memory. I did not argue with Straussman, but hurriedly finished my breakfast and headed to the conference room.

When it was my turn to speak, I read a text from Luke 13: 10-17.

> [10] *On a Sabbath Jesus was teaching in one of the synagogues,*
> [11] *and a woman was there who had been crippled by a spirit for eighteen years. She was bent over and could not straighten up at all.*

> *[12] When Jesus saw her, he called her forward and said to her, "Woman, you are set free from your infirmity."*
> *[13] Then he put his hands on her, and immediately she straightened up and praised God.*
> *[14] Indignant because Jesus had healed on the Sabbath, the synagogue leader said to the people, "There are six days for work. So come and be healed on those days, not on the Sabbath."*
> *[15] The Lord answered him, "You hypocrites! Doesn't each of you on the Sabbath untie your ox or donkey from the stall and lead it out to give it water?*
> *[16] Then should not this woman, a daughter of Abraham, whom Satan has kept bound for eighteen long years, be set free on the Sabbath day from what bound her?"*
> *[17] When he said this, all his opponents were humiliated, but the people were delighted with all the wonderful things he was doing."*

The story of Jesus' teaching on a usual Sabbath morning in a synagogue paints a picture of his meeting a woman who had been afflicted by a spirit of infirmity for eighteen years. The woman's back had been bent, and she was unable to stand up straight as most people would. This woman with her illness was among the congregation listening to Jesus. I imagine that she had been a regular member of that congregation rather than one who had followed Jesus into the church. Jesus saw her. Perhaps the leaders of the synagogue and all the elders knew her too. Jesus called the woman forward.

This was happening in a region where the Jewish temple and synagogues had distinct areas of worship for groups of people, the court of men, the court of women, and the court of Gentiles. The woman would sit in a section where she was allowed, but Jesus was asking her to come to the front. And this was a woman who also had a disability. In the minority groups of that society, she was even more in the minority.

But something happened that day; Jesus saw this woman and called her forward.

It is amazing how, as ministers of the Gospel, and Christians in general, in our preparations to serve the Word of God, often overlook the plight of the people who hurt, but whose plight has become commonplace to such an extent that we cannot see them any longer. We grow immune to their challenge and gradually their pain subsides in our eyes regardless of the hurdles they have to deal with daily.

From Sri Lanka to every country in the world, Jesus Christ has become a shining example to us, and His heart would wish that you and I would not close our eyes to the needs of the people in our communities whose lives are saddled with burdens. Maybe Jesus calls each one of us to be sensitive to this need, rather than conveniently close our ears to their cry.

At a conference where I imagined the participants would be leaving with a renewed zeal to affect the larger world with Christ's gospel of hope, it was jaw-dropping to see how easy it could be to concentrate so much on the delivery of the Gospel and forget the recipients of the Gospel.

When Jesus saw the woman, He called her forward. It is not hard to fathom how this woman, for all the years that she had come to the synagogue, had been sent to the farthest corner of the room so as not to inconvenience the other people. The society had given her a constant affirmation of her unworthiness, and she had no option but to sit on the back bench. Jesus' encounter with her changed her position and changed her setting forever. Perhaps, even if she walked away that day without any miracle in her body, the very fact that she was called from the back to the front caused an incredible change in her emotional posture.

The encounter broke cultural and religious barriers at the time. What difference would we see in our world if whenever the Gospel collides with a culture, it reforms and transforms it into what God would want for us? What a marvelous scene it would be if the healing embrace of the Gospel trumped our perceptions and our attitudes towards people who feel left behind in society! In order for God's glory and the power of God to be seen and felt, it would be an incredible sight if we who overlook the people that society labels as unworthy, were to seize the opportunity to call each of them forward, *to the front*.

Sitting among a group of Christians in Colombo, I couldn't help but think of how urgent it ought to be for the Gospel to confront our theology today, unravel our tradition, and bring a transformation to all of our hearts so that our hands will seek to reach those who stand the farthest off in our communities. If only our doctrines that drive us individually and collectively as a society would be transformed, our journey to uplift the downtrodden, the man with a disability who is unsure of when the next miracle would come, and the afflicted woman who hides her face in the corner of the synagogue, would be one that seeks to bring the glory of Almighty God.

In a population of a little over 20 million, almost two million individuals are documented with some form of disability. In many communities around the world, rather, unfortunately we see any person as person with disability who, as a result of some physical or mental deficiency, is unable to completely provide the basic necessities of life for himself or herself. No one takes the time to distinguish between congenital or otherwise. In other words, in a situation where people are desperate for any help to go through a typical day and live a normal life whether or not they were born with a deficiency or it happened to them is not the focus of attention

The reality in the island of Sri Lanka is no more unique than what exists in our communities and on the streets in Ghana. Approximately three million persons with disabilities in Ghana deal with some form of challenge or another. From physical disability, visual impairment, learning disabilities, to hearing disabilities, there are many more with mental disabilities who were written off a long time ago. People of all ages live through the anguish alone and quietly.

If there were a thought I would be leaving the conference with, it was that a Christian's knowledge of God's word must continually prune the "fig trees" of our lives in order for them to bear good fruits. If Jesus is an example to anyone at all, it is first and foremost to the people who profess the Christian faith, and who live their lives to share the love and grace with which Jesus walked on this earth.

Society will not set the parameters for our faith. It is incredibly important for each of us to pause for a moment and rethink our attitudes toward people who for whatever reason are different from how we are made. Even where there are certain cultures or religions that interpret disability as punishment from God or their own deities, my prayer is that those who profess to be Christians will know better.

I am fascinated by the fact that Jesus healed the woman by stretching forth his hand to touch her. Jesus didn't have to. In fact, there are plenty of examples in the life of Jesus where all he had to do was to speak life or healing into a person. Maybe he touched the woman in this instance because it was significant to paint a picture to the congregation who were looking on. Jesus broke the Jewish tradition and culture of not coming into contact with people who had "blemishes," and were termed "unclean." But did that make Jesus unclean? We find that immediately, the woman stood up straight and praised God. Jesus touched the woman to demonstrate a powerful human connection, one that has sadly found its way out of the church doors in contemporary society.

The irony is that we are representatives of a loving Father whose mercy and love for the social outcast and the marginalized are no less than for anyone else. The same was the case when Jesus touched the leper in a society that had convinced themselves of lepers' unworthiness, and touched the supposedly "dangerous eyes" of the man born blind.

Looking into the eyes of the men and women who had traveled from their own communities to the conference in Sri Lanka, I hoped that we would all be reminded that Jesus is still touching lives today. Jesus, through the hands and feet of you and me, touches the broken and the downtrodden to bring hope and joy to the marginalized. He is touching lives to break barriers so that he will not have many folds, but one complete fold. The best part of the story is that Jesus has put you and me in the ministry of reconciliation, to draw others unto him, regardless of where they have been or how society has defined them.

In the community where the woman received her healing, the ruler of the synagogue displayed unfortunate hypocrisy. It was one that today, cuts deep at the very heart of Christianity. I could only imagine that this owner, an influential man in the community, might have seen this woman several times but never thought of reaching out to make her feel welcome. Yes, he owned the synagogue and that reputation was all that mattered to him, not the human beings who walked through the doors to worship. Interestingly, we see the same man boiling in anger when Jesus healed the woman because it was Sabbath. He only saw that Jesus had healed on the Sabbath. Never mind that he had set a woman free of an infirmity that had gripped her for many years.

Before I laid any blame on the doorstep of this synagogue owner, I am reminded that he probably lived in a society that justified his attitude, so over time he had become numb to the pain of people like the woman. In line with what he had been trained to hold in high esteem, he was probably thinking more of the Sabbath law than of the people that made up his congregation. Could it be that Christians in contemporary society have also walked into this same trap and don't even know it?

In Sri Lanka, I was speaking to people who were relatively influential in their communities, and so the truth probably resonated with them even more. It is rather unfortunate how the louder we claim to stand with the Jesus who went out of His way to heal the broken and mend wounds, the farther we run from the broken and the wounds.

While the world out there reels in pain, and the people who find their way into the churches hide their wounds and pain in the corners, many of us are more concerned with protecting our doctrines and societal norms. We want to protect our positions, even if that means we neglect the very people to whom we are called to minister.

Society's default inclination is to find the people who are more like us, thus making the symbiotic relationship a bit more comfortable. We often have no problem connecting to people with whom we can identify, and we give ourselves every reason under the sun to shy away from the people whose plights are much different from our own. It is no surprise, therefore, that we can afford to be private advocates for people with any kind of disability, while we cannot find the same words to make a difference in public. The encouragement, however, is for Christians to strive to see our fellow human beings like Christ would see them, as opposed to what our social predispositions would have us do.

A few years ago, I was devastated to learn of a minister in a renowned Christian denomination, who was sacked by his church authorities for "wasting" his time on persons with disabilities. As heartbreaking as this sounds, I wondered if the church authorities stopped for a moment to think about what Jesus would do in that situation. Maybe they did what their dogma instructed them to do. The challenge for Christians is not to be consumed with doctrine and dogma to the point where we forget the precious lives at stake in each and every person we come across.

My prayer is for God to make us see through His eyes and open our ears to hear what He would hear. Jesus didn't mince his words when he called the ruler of the synagogue "You hypocrites," because the gatekeepers of the place seemed to have ignored the underlying reason for being there in the first place.

Again, Jesus used the plural "hypocrites" to address the ruler, instead of the singular, "hypocrite." It reminds me of an intriguing thought, albeit an inference, that arose at the conference, that perhaps the ruler had become the spokesperson for the people in the community who didn't care or want to see the woman set free.

Could it be that they were people in no hurry to see another person stand as tall as they were, maybe boosting their own self-importance?

Could it be that the society didn't think it was important to waste their time and resources reaching the people whose burden or disability had tucked them away in the corners of life?

My encounter with Straussman at the conference, and his surprising reaction to my being selected to speak confirmed one thing: that most of us do not walk our talk as Jesus would have us do. It is no wonder then, that we can pay lip service to the disability challenge in every facet of society, even at this highest level, but any energy we have dissipates long before we reach out to the people who need our consideration and care the most.

Could it be that one after another, you and I have drifted into the "hypocrites" category? Could it be that we have become so enamored by religious affiliations that we cannot look past our own comfort zones? God has created humanity in His perfect image, and every one of us is special in our own way to Him. In the case of the woman, she must have been silent throughout the whole encounter. She had probably gone to the same synagogue as she always had, except that Jesus turned the otherwise routine trip into a miraculous turnaround.

The woman didn't have to say a word, because a bigger voice, a powerful voice, a strong voice spoke for her. The voice of Jesus said the words the woman could have said but couldn't have said for herself. Jesus advocated for her, the same way He calls you and me to go into the communities where we can reach the people who have nobody to stand with.

After I had finished delivering the exposition, the message received thunderous applause, perhaps to assure me that I had been able to drum home the message I wanted to put across. After the event, many of the participants walked up to congratulate me. But nothing I had said was to elicit applause. I knew the crisis of the people with disabilities all too well, and I could only encourage my fellow brothers and sisters of faith, from my own experiences.

Bishop Ernesto Murray, the Anglican Bishop of Panama came to me and pleaded on behalf of my friend Jefferson, for forgiveness. I had mentioned him (Jefferson) in my delivery concerning the question he posed to me at the very first day I set my feet at the seminary, "Did the church authorities see you before you were admitted"? I smiled at the Bishop and politely responded that, "I had forgiven him long before now." I only referred to it to make a point, because I sincerely never held a grudge against him. That sentiment lives in the body of Christ everywhere we turn.

As the conference was drawing to a close and we were busily fine-tuning the declarations so far made, Straussman walked straight to me during the tea break, and said, "Brother Cromwell, I am sorry; I apologize for my conduct this morning." Though I accepted his apology, and immediately patched up with him, it dawned on me that unless the world put away its hypocrisy, the fight for recognition, inclusion, respect, and dignity for the marginalized, was going to be a daunting task.

That afternoon, the conference officially came to a close, with a strong conviction of holding *diakonia* as a primary expression of the churches' participation in the ongoing mission of God: re-imagine *diakonia*, and explore *diakonia* from the vantage point of the global South where the dynamics of life are radically different.

Three months after the Colombo Conference, I shared my thoughts on *diakonia* with Jessie, a co-participant from Nigeria. My thoughts were:

> *Reflecting deeply on the Colombo Conference on Diakonia, what I can say is that all this while our churches, I mean African churches, have been doing general diakonia, i.e., the provision of schools and hospitals to our communities. This general diakonia in fact, did help the African continent in time past and continues today.*
>
> *Those who led the independent struggles in various countries in Africa, most of them, were products of mission schools set up by the churches. Dr. Kwame Nkrumah of Ghana*

for instance, was educated in a Catholic school. And so, indirectly, diakonia, embarked on by the missionaries and the churches, became a liberative tool in the hands of the African. The churches therefore have pursued this type of diakonia up to today. But you will hear with me that now we have other agencies providing this type of social services to our people. The biggest stakeholder in this is the state or the government. There are other private individuals and non-governmental organizations in this area. In fact, in most cases, the state has taken over these institutions of the churches, or has partnered with the churches, thereby lessening the churches' impact. For instance, in all public mission schools here in Ghana, it is the government that pays the teachers, and, "He who pays the piper, calls the tune."

If the churches in Africa therefore want to be unique in their diakonia, especially in this 21st century, then they have to embrace what I will term "Specialised Diakonia." Specialized Diakonia is where the diakonia targets persons with special needs. This group includes persons with disabilities, drug addicts, persons with HIV/AIDS, etc. This is a fallow ground that has not been explored by the churches. The church is also a place for the weak and the frail, and not only for the survival of the fittest.

After the Colombo Conference, I became convinced that this is the type of diakonia African churches, including the Presbyterian Church, must pursue. This, I know, will not be easy for individual churches because of the cost of establishing and running such institutions, and there is therefore the need for a concerted effort by the churches to overcome such challenges. African churches need to pool resources together, in order to prove tough in this area.

As a physically challenged person, I look forward to the realization of this dream. In fact, I left Colombo with a strong conviction that Specialized Diakonia should be a priority of the church to make the world a better place for the marginalized.

Having received the mail, Jessie wrote back to me very excited, saying,

Thank you so much, Joseph. This is a truly fine reflection. Please let me have your permission to quote part of the second paragraph verbatim, in which case, I will like to receive your full titles and work designation.

Sincerely
Jessie.

Like Jessie, I also became excited in a sense that the reflection I made had not been in vain, and was helping to re-think *diakonia* to be meaningful in this 21st Century. The challenge, however, was how the people in the communities in which we all live and work would be able to genuinely refrain from latching onto unhealthy stereotypes and determine to reach the men and women and children who are left on the outskirts of life. All of them are masterful creations of Almighty God, and that makes them worthy.

There is often deafening silence in our communities when confronting disability issues becomes the topic for conversation. Rather than being a standard bearer in our communities, and being the one who will uplift Christ's hope in people and places who pray every day for Christ's amazing grace, we are adopting society's patterns of thought and norms. With our words, we often miss the chance to draw one another closer. With our actions, we say over and again that the person whose challenge in life is perhaps much different from our own, is somehow, unworthy.

The mask of religion is what unfortunately doesn't truly change our priorities, passions and our focus. Over and again we all miss the mark, but my prayer is that God continues to orchestrate the affairs of each of our lives to give us the courage to seek opportunities where we can make a difference in the lives of people we walk past or drive by every single day, and whose challenge has become invisible in our hurry to achieve our own dreams.

As Christians, God is counting on us to be a beacon of hope to a world in search of His grace. I believe that we have to be willing to allow God to use us for His glory. It will take our holding on steadfastly to the foundation of our faith to highlight God's unfailing love for the people around us.

CHAPTER

5

A CULTURE IN SEARCH OF A HEART

Myths, Stereotypes and Cultural Attitudes

³⁴ They answered him, "You were born in utter sin, and would you teach us?" And they cast him out. John 9:34.

In June of 2013, I was in Uganda for the All Africa Conference of Churches' Golden Jubilee Assembly. It was held at the Munyonyo Commonwealth Resort, Kampala, Uganda. I had been invited as an observer, courtesy of the Ecumenical Disability Advocates Network (EDAN). I remember the elation of being able to get some insight into how Christians in different parts of the continent were confronting and addressing the various challenges persons with disability face.

I knew how much work the church in Ghana still had left to do, and I imagined others would have unique perspectives on the issue in their own countries. The theme for the conference had been advertised as "God of life; lead Africa to peace, justice, and dignity." The underlying thought was about the Church of God and human dignity.

I listened attentively as one after the other, prominent church leaders took their turns to share their own thoughts. The Most Rev. Professor Emmanuel K. Asante, who at the time was the Presiding Bishop of The Methodist Church Ghana, and who had also been my lecturer at the Trinity Theological Seminary, Professor John Mbiti, a renowned African Christian theologian, and Professor Patrick Loch Otieno Lumumba, the Director at Kenya School of Law, spoke during the official opening. Their inspirational words carefully described some of the challenges in society, but also the urgent need for every Christian to view the world through the loving and restoring eyes of our Heavenly Father.

Little did I know that I would be sharing the same platform with these eminent speakers, until the delegates from the EDAN appointed me to make a presentation on the last day of the conference. I was not on the programme, and as such, did not prepare a special sermon or presentation in advance. Coincidentally, mine was the last activity on the agenda, and I imagined that everybody was tired and perhaps even eager to head home. Nonetheless, I reckoned I would speak briefly, and understandably, since owing to the short notice I had been given, I couldn't do any elaborate presentation.

As it was with any conference or convention, by the last day, participants would be ready to return to their normal lives and be reviewing their travel plans. I prayed that they would find something I said relevant enough to stick around through the entire session. Interestingly, if all the attendees were to remember just one thing, it might very well be the words of the last speaker, in case something I say left an indelible mark on their hearts.

I shared a thought from the verses in Luke 13:10-17. The theme, **"God of life: lead Africa to peace, justice and dignity"** seemed very appropriate for the year's assembly. I found it apt, particularly because it spoke to issues that many people, if not all, with disabilities on the African continent seemed to wrestle with every waking day. The challenges remained, the doctrines and church dialogue were unclear, and in many cases, churches had adapted their theology to social norms and ignored the heart of God and His amazing love.

Ghana's and Africa's reality are no different from that of other parts of the world where to this day, the issue of disability is more than just an individual personal crisis, but a painful exchange with society. In many places I had been, big cities and small villages, there were enough voices whispering in the ears of men and women with disabilities that they were inadequate. Their names have been shamed, and they have had to fight through the host of voices that tell them their lives are a mistake and even a curse.

That afternoon, as I stood in front of all the people who had gathered for the conference, I couldn't help but reiterate a simple prayer, that the God of all life would instruct all our hearts in our homes and towns and villages not to let unfounded myths shape our attitudes towards our brothers and sisters, sons and daughters, and every person whose life we touch or whose plight we see.

The Jesus we find in the Gospel of Luke is the man who saw people at their lowest ebb and found a way to restore them to the best that they could become.

Many women and men have to fight a daily battle with the stereotypes and the perceptions that have been entrenched in society to such extent that no one cares to wonder where they come from in the first place. For a society so confident that we are civilized and enlightened, we have continued to throw reason out of the window and latch on to archaic interpretations molded by cultural practices.

Maybe, at least in the case of Africa, poverty probably makes it easier to buy into a stereotype than deal with it. Even for issues that we can address head-on, we elect for the option that allows us to find comfortable excuses.

Persons with disabilities have been treated variously by organized religions and cultures. These religions and cultures express contradictory views of whether persons with disability should be shunned, punished, eradicated or aided, with some people even arguing that persons with disabilities should be viewed not as citizens with equal rights, but as objects of welfare, health and charity programmes. These reactions have come about due to the cultural transpositions of the people, i.e., underlying assumptions, beliefs, and ideas that are generally shared but not defined, because they are obvious to those who hold them. These views seem to have affected the ways physically challenged people have been viewed and treated socially and religiously.

This reminds me of an incident that happened to me in one of the universities in Ghana, between 2000 and 2002. At the time I was pursuing my theological education at Trinity Theological Seminary, Legon-Accra. I had, one afternoon, gone to the University of Ghana, Legon-Accra, which was not far from the Seminary, to go and look for Phyllis, who had come back to her "alma mater" to pursue her Master's degree. Phyllis was the wife of my cousin, Emmanuel Nortey. Emma and I grew up together and we are more than cousins—in fact, we are friends. We completed Sixth Form in the same year, though from different schools.

On reaching Phyllis' Hall, I climbed the staircase leading to her room, which was on the first floor. I knocked at the door to her room, and a voice not familiar to me responded, asking me to enter. When I entered I saw a lady, supposedly Phyllis' roommate, resting on her bed. Before I could ask about Phyllis' whereabouts, this young lady started screaming leaving me in a state of confusion and embarrassment. To avoid any misrepresentation and further chagrin, I immediately left the scene and went back to my campus.

As I lay on my bed that evening, I started asking myself what would have caused that lady to behave the way she behaved. Hasn't she ever come across a person with disability before? Why did she scream when I had not posed the slightest threat to her? Or did my mere presence pose a threat when she had not yet known about my mission of coming there? What would have happened to me, if her mates in the Hall had heard her scream and had come to her defense? Who would be there to defend me, when the only person I knew in the Hall, Phyllis was not around? And who would be there to listen to my side of the story?

I was almost in tears, and I told myself, "Disability is a struggle; a struggle from all facets of life." Like Mary Magdalene who was heading towards the tomb of the Lord Jesus Christ on the dawn of the Resurrection morning, I prayed, "Who will roll this stone away for us"? May God have mercy! I never made any attempt again to visit Phyllis. Enough of that intimidation and embarrassment!

It is easy to label people with specific physical or mental disabilities as unproductive members of society. Even as Christians, most of us are trained from childhood to avoid anything that is evil and not from God. As excellent as that indoctrination is, it becomes a problem when culture and society define sin for us, and entrenched traditions shape our worldview toward sin. When we are needed to stand in the gap and intercede, we hide behind the curtain of culture and traditions and shun the people who probably need help the most. In our effort to keep our distance from the "unclean" we become more like the world, and less like the light that is supposed to illuminate it.

The sad reality is that the expectations imposed both consciously and unconsciously on society tell the person with disability not to even try to see himself/herself any differently. Within a society that expects a person to be more than a burden, people respond and act accordingly. If we are to stand as Christians, we have to be disciples of a Jesus who didn't stop healing the broken, comforting the afflicted and rebuilding lives simply because the culture at the time demanded otherwise.

Perhaps Jesus knew how conveniently human nature runs to use culture and norms as a crutch for avoiding the things we want to stay away from. When the task at hand is uncomfortable, most of us find an escape in latching on to society's expectations to define our actions. That was not the case for Jesus. His perfect love and steadfast grace wouldn't let Him.

In Jesus' profound encounter with the man who had spent much of his life in a place he wished he wouldn't have been — by the pool of Bethesda — the environment didn't have any impact on his feeling toward the man. Jesus didn't pause to wonder whether it was acceptable to talk to the sick man; it didn't make a difference to him. Jesus didn't pause to wonder what the onlookers at the place they called the Sheep Gate would think about him if he attempted to heal the man; their opinions were of no consequence to him. In fact, Jesus knew all the rules of his society, and was well aware of the customs, but the man's pain was much more important to him than custom. This is a remarkable example to every one of us, that our hearts ought not to be so entrenched in our culture that we look past our brothers' and sisters' plight.

Jesus gave up everything to save the world he loved, and that didn't exclude the person whom society had branded "unworthy." Perhaps for months and years, all the man had heard was how pitiful his life had become, and even if no one said that out loud for him to hear, many people may have shunned him enough times so that he couldn't help but read their minds. The man had been in his condition for 38 years, and there probably weren't many people walking by who shared an encouraging word. For 38 long years, he had felt the dejection from his own kinsmen/women; thank God he encountered Jesus, who changed his situation by healing him and restoring his dignity.

I think about how Jesus saw a woman in the congregation and didn't let culture hold him back from reaching her at her lowest point. In a community that perhaps had looked down on her plight for at least 18 years, Jesus was very much aware that not everyone would applaud his actions. For people in our churches and neighborhoods who are running to the touch of Jesus Christ, can you and I have the boldness to feel their frustrations and share in their challenges?

Can you and I respond to the call of Christ to not let the cultural norms we have grown accustomed to, build a wall around the people who have been denigrated and shunned by our society? The woman's dignity was restored, and I could imagine what she felt, knowing that someone who didn't have to, had gone out of his way to break away from the myths and the stereotypes that defined attitudes.

One thing Jesus knew standing in the midst of the people who were set in their ways, and had even convinced themselves of their own righteousness, was that his heart was driven by God's love for the woman, rather than by what society dictated. The powerful example is for Christians in every part of the world to recognize the unique power we have through our Lord Jesus Christ to heal broken hearts. The miracle is not always an outward manifestation of change. That is the work of the Holy Spirit, but you and I can do our part to help uplift the people who are left to carry the weight of society's rejection.

With the physical touch alone, perhaps seemingly insignificant to most of us, Jesus broke the Jewish tradition whereby persons with disabilities were seen as sinners and needed to be avoided. The cry of the woman's heart was much more important to him than the disapproving looks of the people who had gathered in the room.

Persons with disabilities on the African continent, like the Jewish woman with the bent back, have been marginalized for many years, even by some sections of the church and humanity. Perhaps before we are pronounced guilty of hypocrisy and not walking in the footsteps of Christ, we must truly reexamine how far we stand from the people who need our healing hands and uplifting words the most. In the passage, the woman's voice was not heard, but thank God, Jesus spoke for her. He was (and still is) the voice of the voiceless.

All of us can begin the probably unpopular journey of emulating Christ's example by advocating for persons with disabilities, rather than conveniently piling a weight of cultural expectations on them.

It so happens that for Christians, there has always been a need for a person's life to be free of blemishes. What the early church came to consider as a blemish, is pretty distant from what we have come to understand in contemporary society where we are fortunate to understand the medical roots of many conditions people face. Unfortunately, even armed with all this knowledge, we are caught in a society where it is more convenient to alienate than to embrace, to cast away instead of extending an invitation.

Many researchers have pointed to the reality in the Orthodox and Catholic Churches where there happened to be clear statements of doctrine, opposing ministry by persons with physical disabilities. One such researcher, Harold H. Wilke mentioned how the Catholic doctrine included *admiratio populi* — referring to discomfort among members of the congregation in response to a public figure whose outward appearance could be distracting. In Protestant as well as Catholic circles, a clergyperson was understood to be the one for others. This upfront role, enacted before the congregation, was of course very public: administering the sacraments, preaching the word, and being of service to other human beings within and without the congregation.

If societal attitudes are to change, it will take very intentional steps from any arena of society that is willing to address the stigma attached to disabilities and challenge our interpretation of our customs. If any segment of society can respond more positively to physical and all other forms of disability, it will be men and women in the Christian faith for whom the message of grace and restoration ought to be their guiding light.

For this reason, I have always been confident that churches can play an instrumental role in helping remove obstacles in the way of persons with disabilities, so that they also can answer positively to the call of God. It is not culture's task to dictate our mandate on earth. Our focus should be on God's unchanging word, one that extends grace to all people regardless of how far down they have fallen, or how much society has rendered them unworthy.

CHAPTER

6

TRADING PLACES

Every Life has a Story

⁹Some said, "It is he"; others said, "No, but he is like him."
He said, "I am the man." John 9:9.

One day my granny asked me "Joe, do you know why the hen sometimes draws one of its legs into its feathers and stands on the other?" "No, Granny," I replied. She then told me that the hen was anticipating a time when a world emperor would rise up and make a decree that all right legs of hens be amputated. "So when you see a hen standing on one leg, then it is practicing how it will be able to live or cope when that edict is passed," she concluded.

At the moment Granny was telling me this story, little did I know that she was teaching me a great lesson about disability. Disability is universal; it affects both humans and animals. The hen is figuring out how it can live and still make life meaningful should it happen that one of its legs is amputated. It is also figuring out how some of its kind which are already in that predicament go about their lives. This would give it a better understanding of what they deal with.

It is often almost impossible to truly imagine someone's pain, simply because no matter how hard we try, there is no way to truly recreate the challenge the other person has to live with every day and every night. The challenge with which they live with for so long that it eventually becomes their lot in life. It becomes their normal way of life because there is really no way of escaping that reality. It is impossible to imagine not being able to do the simplest things that most of us take for granted. What is easy may be a giant hurdle to someone else. The hen has a lot to teach us and we must embrace it with all humility.

It is like a mother of a newborn baby, who cannot comprehend the miracle of her child's good health until she walks across the Intensive Care Unit of a hospital and see the faces of many helpless babies who would do anything to trade places with the child she carries in her arms. The mother's heart would feel the pain of the children in the little cribs, with tubes tied to their little hands and nostrils, who are unable to fend for themselves. Maybe it is the mother's knowing that the children are completely helpless causes her to feel empathy for these little strangers. Maybe her knowing the little babies' stories is why it is easy for her to send a smile their way or say a little prayer on their behalf.

In our own communities, there are many people walking through our streets feeling neglected and overwhelmed by the weight of what they have to deal with. If society didn't already label them as unworthy and worthless, their families abandoned them a long time ago and assigned a shame label to them. The years of scorn and living through whatever challenges they had to endure piled enough pressure on them to give up on themselves.

Can you imagine yourself trading places with this person, even for a moment? When we pause and quietly think about what we would do without God's grace or where we would be if God's grace didn't guide our every step, we would be slow to cast off another person, created in Almighty God's image, with whom we could have easily traded places and lived our lives in their shoes. Jesus traded places with the poor, the sick and the social outcasts, and expects his followers to do same.

In the Parable of the sheep and goats (Matthew 25:31-46), Jesus commended and rewarded the righteous for trading places with the poor, the sick, the migrants, and prisoners, equating them to himself. On the other hand, those who did not trade places with the poor, the sick, the migrants, and the prisoners were punished and condemned to eternal fire. To identify with the social outcast is to identify with Christ.

At the heart of the tradition and community at the time was one flaw: that perhaps people didn't find any value in stopping for a moment to imagine the journey that may have brought people to a particular point in their lives. Society will not ordinarily do so, but as Christians we ought to operate with a different lens through which we see every individual as being worth our time and our prayer. They are worthy to our Almighty Father.

Indeed every person has his/her own story, some more striking than others but none of less value. Maybe the person who carries the weight of society on his shoulders saw his dreams and hopes vanish like smoke in the air. The doubts turn into disillusionment, and slowly the years turn into a time filled with uncertainty. God doesn't write us off because of it.

The powerful thing about the opportunity to share grace with the people we meet, persons with disability whom some cultures find it so easy to shove to the side because their voices are not loud enough to scream for attention, is that it is comforting to know that the love that is rooted in God's abundant grace doesn't require their cries for attention. God hears every one of us, and the blind man's life is not of less value because of what he cannot see.

Jesus met the blind man when many in the Jewish community at the time had concluded that the man was born in sin and that his plight was a direct result of something evil. Maybe someone should have reminded them that none of them was so special or important that it could not have been them in that situation. Maybe they forgot a powerful truth: that it is only through God's grace that all of us go back and forth through our day and through life, not because of some special status we have attained. Certainly, it was not because of some righteousness from which we've been born.

No wonder, even after Jesus had performed the miracle of healing the man, the most ardent of critics were the man's neighbors. We would imagine they would have been the happiest to see him healed. But they did not trade places with him, even when he was healed. The tensions in the relationships between the blind man and his neighbors were no different from what all of us have experienced in our societies.

Jesus, our great and unflinching example, was willing to take center stage to demonstrate a love that disregards status. Each one of us, in every station of life, has a chance to see the next person through a lens that is slow to judge, slow to write off another person's potential, and label a person as worthless.

In Jesus's day, some scholars found in John's gospel had a theology that didn't allow them to extend grace to a person whose condition they didn't readily understand, and whose plight they thought was probably much different from their own. The Jews at the time saw such conditions as the blind man's the way their religion and culture had instructed them. One of such groups was the Pharisaic group, the well-known Pharisees — who were at loggerheads with Jesus for having performed a miracle on the man born blind. The Pharisees belonged to the Jewish authorities who were responsible for excluding people from the synagogue whom they considered unworthy.

The intriguing observation is that they probably overlooked the significance of the miracle because it was a reality that was not theirs, and a plight they could hardly fathom. Could it be, perhaps if it was their own son or daughter who needed the healing touch of Jesus, they wouldn't have challenged Jesus the way they did?

In an article, "The Signs as Witnesses in the Fourth Gospel: Reexamining the Evidence," I ran across the thought of how "signs" (σημεία) played a central role in the community of Jesus' day. It is noteworthy, however, that no matter the magnitude of the signs that the people witnessed, they were not willing to deviate from their deeply entrenched attitudes towards the people they had predetermined as unfit to be welcomed with open arms.

A prevailing school of thought explained how, when it came to the persons with disability, as in the case of the man born blind, the debate often hovered on the religious perception of blindness which led to the "Jewish" judgement of the person. The issue with the Pharisees who condemned Jesus's decision to heal the man on a Sabbath day goes beyond a Sabbath controversy and borders more on perceptions and relational ties towards persons with disabilities. There is probably no way of knowing how the Pharisees would have responded if that healing happened to someone of their own families who desperately needed a miracle or the touch of Almighty God.

In his fascinating article, "No Steps to Heaven," Harold H. Wilke, Director of the Healing Community, a program of the New Samaritan Corporation, told a story concerning the then President of Union Theological Seminary. Once he sat in a wheelchair in an effort to put himself in the place of a student with disability. For a moment, Harold Wilke wanted to walk in the shoes of the people he had been called to serve, and the only way, he reasoned, was to live a moment travelling the same paths they did.

He recounted the difficulties he went through as two of his students tried assisting him. This experience pointed out a striking reality to him, that in an American society where 10 to 15 per cent of the population were persons with a range of disabilities, there was still an enormous amount of work to be done for their plight to be truly accounted for, recognized, before even an attempt would be made to address them.

The phenomenon is even direr across Africa and other parts of the world, where a cultural overlay allows this reality to be relegated to the background even further. Someday, I pray that societies will rise up to the challenge of caring for our brothers and sisters whose mental and physical disabilities leave them at the mercy of anyone but themselves, or whose ability to push through the daily grind is hampered by obstacles. Until then, the Church will have the responsibility to address any such barriers, both attitudinal and structural. In this way, the Church needs to take it upon itself to educate its members and the general society, to readily accept persons with disabilities as one of their own and accord them with the full status available to every citizen.

The Church has a great responsibility to affect society's attitude positively, to remove the negative tag most societies have put on persons with disabilities. To do this effectively, the church must have a structure or policy on disability to guide it. It is quite unfortunate that this is lacking in most churches. It is high time the church rose to the task.

Arie Rimmerman is a professor of Social Welfare and Social Planning, and the head of the School of Social Work at the University of Haifa, Israel. Speaking of the reality of persons with disabilities from his own cultural context, in "Israel's Equal Rights for Persons with Disabilities Law: Current Status and Future Direction," he expressed how people with disabilities were more often than not, viewed not as citizens with legal rights like anyone else, but as objects of welfare, health, and charity programs. Their value is instinctively reduced to nothing, and seen as a problem that needs to be resolved, and a burden that needs to be managed.

From his vantage point, Rimmerman reasoned that unfortunately, it was that kind of social policy approach — one that at best consisted of reactive and piecemeal responses to specific social conditions — that contributed indirectly to the segregation of persons with disabilities from their mainstream society into special schools, sheltered workshops, and housing. Subsequently, and probably against what the culture would readily accept, individuals continued to call for a human rights approach to disability law and social policy against a background of specific entitlements and other social policy provisions found primarily in the areas of health, rehabilitation, transportation, education and employment.

In most societies around the world, the sad reality happens over and over again where the exclusion and segregation of persons with disabilities are accepted as the norm. Of course, there are many arenas where the mistreatment of people is frowned upon or even in many cases blatantly condemned, but the questions arise about the honesty of our intentions when we do so only in those scenarios we find most comfortable.

Often, any recognition tends to be a result of political choices based on false assumptions about people with disabilities in an able-bodied society. It may be most helpful for the focus to shift from viewing disability as an individual problem to defining it as a failure of society to consider human differences and challenges.

There is now a global growing concern towards disability issues and the Church needs not be left out of this. Indeed, it is expected to take a leading role to aid persons with disabilities. The time is now for a wake-up call for the body of Christ to stand in the truth set out by God's word, rather than to let the tenets of culture define our attitudes and actions.

Persons with disabilities have been treated as objects of charity, welfare and health programs for far too long, and not as citizens with rights. Again, religion, including Christianity, has contributed to the negative plight of persons with disabilities.

At the heart of the discussion would have to be the basic truths about all of us, not only from a religious viewpoint but using a human approach with love and grace, to accept every person as having been created by God in His own image.

There are records from the ancient Babylonian civilization, around 2000 B.C.E., that indicated that Semitic Chaldean diviners of the future maintained a list of "birth deformities" and specific prophetic meanings connected to each. Thus, the births of children with impairments were used to predict the future.

In such an environment, a person's future was defined from the first day, and there was no opportunity for him or her to lead the fulfilling life to which Almighty God had called him/her.

Empathy and a genuine respect for treating people who live with one form of obstacle or another doesn't automatically happen. In fact, the social reality that confronts people with various forms of disabilities is nothing new.

Throughout history, there are countless examples of individuals and communities who go to extreme lengths to marginalize people whom they considered outcasts. It was only when the proverbial shoe "ended up on the other foot", that they would be forced to see life through another person's eyes.

CHAPTER

7

WHAT WOULD JESUS DO?
Taking Action.

⁶As he said this, he spat on the ground and made clay of the spittle and anointed the man's eyes with the clay. John 9:6.

I have been fortunate to live most of my life as a Christian, and there is nothing in this world that gives me greater joy and peace than having Christ as my savior, my friend, and my life's focus. I had the chance to be in the company of many men and women who profess Christ to be their savior, yet struggle to express the same love in action that Jesus spent his life teaching.

Along the way, I also uncovered some of the rather unflattering realities about groups whose worldview affects many, but who seldom seem to pause to imagine how their words and actions cut at the core of another's life. Occasionally, I have had to stop and wonder how such doctrines came to be, and how comfortable Jesus would be if he sat in our midst.

For some Christians, and in fact tracing from the pre-Christianity era, the Old Testament stories have served as blueprints on how we relate to people with disabilities. Often we have acted on what we believed in our hearts to be the right thing to do. We found references in the Bible that associated disability with sin, and missed the heart of Jesus and his amazing grace completely, so that in many cases what jumped to the forefront were verses that shaped our religious attitudes.

A recent encounter with a few church leaders was striking. I had been invited to come and talk on "Ministering to Persons with Disabilities." In the midst of seasoned theologians, I decided to solicit their views on one of the difficult passages in the Old Testament, as far as disability is concerned.

Leviticus 21: 16-23:

> *"16 The Lord said to Moses,*
> *17 "Say to Aaron: 'For the generations to come none of your descendants who has a defect may come near to offer the food of his God.*
> *18 No man who has any defect may come near: no man who is blind or lame, disfigured or deformed;*
> *19 no man with a crippled foot or hand,*
> *20 or who is a hunchback or a dwarf, or who has any eye defect, or who has festering or running sores or damaged testicles.*
> *21 No descendant of Aaron the priest who has any defect is to come near to present the food offerings to the Lord. He has a defect; he must not come near to offer the food of his God.*
> *22 He may eat the most holy food of his God, as well as the holy food;*
> *23 yet because of his defect, he must not go near the curtain or approach the altar, and so desecrate my sanctuary. I am the Lord, who makes them holy.'"*

Chapter 7: What Would Jesus Do?

As I gave the Ministers the opportunity to comment on the text, three main schools of thoughts emerged
- The view that the passage might be a later insertion, and might not be part of the original text;
- The opinion that the text was an integral part of the Torah (the Law, which is the Five Books of Moses), yet the coming of our Lord Jesus Christ to bestow grace on us, had rendered that entire passage barring persons with disabilities from entering into priesthood, inoperative. They supported this position with Old Testament rituals and festivals which are no longer celebrated on the Christian calendar;
- The affirmation of the validity of that text, further arguing that God knew why he barred persons with disabilities from ministering in His presence, and the church must adhere to that.

After the lengthy discussions, I decided to probe into some of the ideas expressed, to see whether they would stand the test of time. I began by inquiring into how people are called into the ministry. It emerged that, in most cases, it was the individual who underwent certain experiences, and got convinced that God was calling him for a higher service. When that fact was established, I told them my own experiences, which had convinced me that God was calling me into the ministry. If a person without a disability could go through certain experiences and convince himself of God's calling on him, I didn't see why a person with a disability, who goes through a similar experience, would be blocked from becoming a priest.

Further, priesthood is no longer following the Aaronic line. At the coming of the Lord Jesus Christ, a new order of priesthood was created: the Order of Melchizedek.

> *[11] If perfection could have been attained through the Levitical priesthood—and indeed the law given to the people established*

> *that priesthood—why was there still need for another priest to come, one in the order of Melchizedek, not in the order of Aaron?* ¹² *For when the priesthood is changed, the law must be changed also . . .* ¹⁸ *The former regulation is set aside because it was weak and useless* ¹⁹ *(for the law made nothing perfect), and a better hope is introduced, by which we draw near to God.*
>
> Hebrews 7:11-12, 18-19.

The Levitical priesthood could not establish any perfection, though persons with disabilities were barred from entering into it. With this statement in Hebrews, what would you say caused the imperfection? Was it our sinful nature?

Moreover, I drew the attention of the participants to the eye defect as a basis for disqualifying persons to become priests, as found in Leviticus 21:20, *"or who is a hunchback or a dwarf, or who has any eye defect, or who has festering or running sores or damaged testicles."* I paused and looked straight into the eyes of these ministers and told them, "I am sorry, by this text, most of you do not qualify to become God's Ministers, for you have disabilities in your eyes; you wear glasses."

The whole auditorium burst into laughter, for more than half of the participants there were wearing glasses, and it had never occurred to them that they had fallen into the disability bracket. It was at this point that many came to realize that disability was part of humankind, and they should also use the pulpit and any available media to advocate for persons with disabilities. Though I do not pray that you become a person with disability, I also don't want to hide that fact of life from you.

Over the years, I have come across some Christians who hold the notion that persons with disabilities are burdened with some sickness or infirmity. They argued fervently and passionately about their view that any person with some physical or mental disability needed to be healed by all means. They needed to be restored and be made whole. A person being whole in our own minds is what fits into our sense, regardless of the purpose for which a person walks the face of the earth.

There have even been cases where members of the church would see persons with disabilities as people whose inability to receive healing is evidence of a much larger issue: a lack of faith in Jesus. Unfortunately, persons with disabilities get hurt when branded as portraying lack of faith in God. In my own journey through the Christian faith, I have found how easily people tend to ignore the broader view of healing. In an effort to interpret their own faith through their spiritual lenses, they make the error of only laying emphasis on physical healing.

It was particularly intriguing, even in Jesus' encounter with the blind man that the negative perceptions of the man's neighbors didn't change immediately even after he received his healing. Jesus' ultimate concern for healing the congenitally blind man was to lead him to faith. The physical healing therefore was a means to an end, and not an end in itself, hence Jesus' second encounter with the man, when he led him to faith. I can only imagine that if Jesus walked in our communities today, he would challenge all of us to work diligently in every area where we can, to build bridges and heal hearts that ache as a result of society's negative attitudes.

Throughout the social context of the Bible's New Testament, I stumbled across places where I found that the attitude of people at the time, towards persons with disabilities had not been the most admirable. There are many well-documented instances where religious leaders seemed to be more concerned about the observance of Sabbath rituals than about seeing the glory of God restored in the hearts of men and women whom society had labelled as outcasts.

In the Gospel of Luke 6:7, I could only imagine the pain of a man with a withered hand whose faith and hope was crushed by religious people who thought the observance of the Sabbath's rituals was much more important than Jesus' restoration of a broken life. The Bible recounts the story of the man desperately seeking the attention of Jesus, but a crowd sternly ordering him to keep quiet (Luke 18:38-39). Ironically, his own people became an impediment when he wanted to get to Jesus, the "Son of David." It was remarkable to imagine how we allow our own interpretation of life's events to define our expectations of other people.

Another intriguing story in the Bible, as the Gospel of John tells, is of a man who seemed to not have the strength to outrun others to get into the pool where he believed he could be healed. The story shares how the people believed that an angel at particular season would stir a pool in Jerusalem by a place known as the Sheep Gate, so that any person with any disease who stepped in the water first, would be healed. Many sick people, men and women who were either blind or paralyzed in some form, would wait for their chance for a miracle. Unfortunately, this man didn't have anyone to help him get into the pool in time for any miracle. It was not until Jesus showed up on the scene that everything changed.

The Jewish laws, therefore, informed the thoughts and actions of these events found in the New Testament, and as Jews, the people in the Gospels were not going to absolve persons with disabilities from sin. This approach to disability affected the worship life of people like the congenital blind man and became a hindrance to his religious experience.

The general perception was that sin was the main cause of disability. In that case, people of faith resigned themselves to the only thing they were allowed to do—lead a secluded life. The views of the community in those years, strangely, has not changed at all in contemporary society, even though we have learned much more throughout history, and most importantly, since grace through Christ Jesus ought to be our guiding light.

The story of the man who had been blind from birth was such that he faced a lot of resistance in his own community. Even after he had been healed by Jesus, some of his own neighbors failed to recognize him and the Jews also excommunicated him. His community, therefore, did not even attempt to have a good relationship with him, and did not share in his joy at receiving his sight. He went through a lot of interrogations at the hands of the Pharisees, and the Jews tried to discredit his claim of being cured by Jesus. All the characters in this narrative (excluding Jesus) treated the congenitally blind man as a social outcast.

But Jesus' attitude towards this man was contrary to the attitude of the people in this community. After the man had been excommunicated, Jesus went to look for him and had more interactions with him. Jesus disclosed himself to the man born blind as the Son of Man and led the man born blind to worship him. Could it be that Jesus portrayed a friendly attitude towards the man born blind against the norm of the Jewish Community, because he saw the man's heart, while the rest of the community could not get past what his former physical condition?

It comes as no surprise that religious people of different denominations find Bible verses a basis for their opinions. What becomes conveniently relegated into the background is the social context within which the statement was made, or the instruction was given. Even more intriguing is how in many arenas in contemporary society, all of us forget that under the same law as in Old Testament times, none of us would qualify to stand in the presence of Almighty God, for it was only the Aaronic line that qualified to be chosen as priests. Now grace abounds for all.

One of the most discouraging outcomes of modern church practices is that they find a way of pushing away the people in our communities who live with one disability or another. People who met their miracles when they met Jesus weren't free of such rejection; even when the miracle occurred, the stigma stayed behind.

Without much effort, people who have had to live with any disability become objects of pity and charity, even inside of the four walls of the church.

Sadly, as Christians in contemporary society we often take on the label and leave behind the heart of compassion rooted in the love and grace of Jesus Christ. Our communities ridicule and alienate persons with disabilities with our words and our actions. This is in striking contrast to what Jesus, whose name we have chosen to carry, would have done. There is nothing that stops us all from encouraging people to see beyond their limitations. There is no decree that says Christians cannot pray for the hurting, or cannot pass on encouraging words to people who we reckon need them. The challenge is in response to a simple question, after the prayer and the exhortation—what else? What further steps do we take after we have done all the spiritual work and trusted God to do the healing and the restoration? What would our Lord Jesus Christ do?

The story about Jesus' encounter with the man born blind and the rippling effect of this encounter in the Jewish community is relevant today, in almost every corner of the world. There have been schools of thought that argue that since the Jews of the time mostly practiced Judaism, they must have resisted any form of religious doctrine that seemed to contradict what they had believed all of their lives.

The healing of the congenitally blind man was supposed to be a confirmation of Jesus' teaching on his being the "light of the world"—an identifier the community couldn't fit into their belief system. Jesus became a remarkable example to all of us through his actions and genuine compassion for anyone who reached out to him. His arms were open for an embrace that reassured anyone that they too were indeed worthy.

All of us, in our communities, and regardless of the prominence of our actions, can also become the light of the world, and find opportunities to bring hope to aching hearts, and see our fellow human beings, irrespective of their physical or mental conditions, with a heart of grace.

What would Jesus do? I will not doubt that any time he encountered men and women whom society had shunned and pushed aside, he would pray with them. But I am also convinced that his ministry to them would not end with a prayer. My best guess is that Jesus would touch the lives of the people he meets, and change their stories. From the examples he set through his own life, we know a Jesus who would go out of his way to help someone. Can we go out of our way to touch a life with a kind word or a helping hand? Can we be pushed out of our comfort zones even for a moment to do as Jesus would?

Across the world, no matter how many people dare to live beyond their physical, mental or emotional challenges, there has always been the prevailing misconception that anyone with any such handicaps is inevitably fruitless and perhaps just waiting their turn on line for charity. These misconceptions have defined attitudes and continue to shape expectations.

> ² *And his disciples asked him, "Rabbi, who sinned, this man, or his parents that he was born blind"?* ³ *Jesus answered, "It was not that this man sinned, or his parents, but that the works of God might be made manifest in him."*

Often when I recall the story, I imagine a scene where Jesus' answer might have come as a disappointment or surprise to his disciples. These were men who spent most of their waking days with Jesus, during their discipleship; the presence of Jesus didn't automatically strip away their conditioned attitude and beliefs.

The disciples may have thought they were being helpful by offering Jesus suggestions on how he ought to respond to the man born blind. Interestingly, none of the possible answers suggested to him was selected, and it was not too hard to understand why. Having come from a community where a certain attitude was upheld and every one had been consciously or even unconsciously indoctrinated to think along the same lines, it was not surprising to hear their unanimous interpretation of the person's disability. They didn't see the man as Jesus saw him.

The disciples didn't see beyond the societal perception enough to understand that no matter the seeming imperfection, a person's value in the eyes of Almighty God is never tainted, and certainly never diminished. Maybe this scenario in itself is an absorbing reminder to all of us Christians that we could stand in the presence of Jesus, and still be programmed by our society's norms and attitudes.

It is remarkable how Jesus, having dismissed sin as the cause of the man's blindness, did not stop there. He went even further to give the cause of the man's blindness saying, *". . . but that the works of God be made manifest in him."*

By attributing the cause of the man's blindness to the works of God that needed to be manifested, Jesus reminded all of us to refrain from attributing events to causes that we know nothing of, and not to be inclined to assume a generational curse to have played a role in a person's life.

When society looked at a man at a low point in his life and wrote him off for his disability, Jesus saw the best in him. Jesus saw a man created in the image of Almighty God and a person whose destiny was not curbed because of his disability.

Even when the world can only see a person's limitation or even what they qualify as the worst part of his/her life, Jesus leaves a shining example for you and I to remember that nothing in this life can strip us of the worth he has already bestowed on us.

Jesus debunked the position of attributing the man's situation to sin, as he declared that "It was not that this man sinned or his parents . . ." Though this first part of Jesus' answer exonerated the man and his parents from being held responsible for the blindness, it began the conflict that was to characterize what followed. Was the exoneration enough to settle the issue once and for all? Did Jesus himself not tell the man healed at the Pool of Bethesda to go and sin no more? (John. 5:14).

In view of this, were the disciples therefore not right in alluding to sin as the cause of the man's blindness?

It was always incredibly powerful to find Jesus in a teaching moment where he was not biased towards persons with disabilities and would rebuke where rebuke was necessary. So if on the one hand he told the man at the Pool of Bethesda to go and sin no more, and on another, exonerated the man born blind from sin, could it be that Jesus was responding to specific situations in the lives of the people he met, and just as he saw past their outward appearance, he was ministering to their hearts in a way the people around could never have understood?

My own prayer is that we continue to ask God to give us sight beyond what we can physically see. For in our own eyes, our instincts will not automatically push us to react to the world around us as God would have us do. My prayer is that we can have the strength and courage to see life beyond our immediate horizon and reach out to our brothers and sisters whose plight may have quelled their voices, and left their hopes fragile and on the verge of being crushed. Just as God alone sees the heart of a person, only He can reach a person in a way that truly makes him/her whole. All we have been called to do is to emulate Christ's perfect example and love and share His amazing grace to the ends of the world.

One of the beautiful examples of God's power is the fact that God's ways are not like our own, and inasmuch as we would love to understand His reasoning for why things happen and to whom those things happen, we will never have a mind magnificent enough to comprehend all that He alone can. God is asking you and me only to do our part to embrace the person He has created, and leave the parts we cannot understand to Him alone.

That is what Jesus would have done.

CHAPTER

8

DIFFERENT ON PURPOSE

Grace to Rewrite Our Story

⁷saying to him, "Go, wash in the pool of Siloam" (which means Sent). So he went and washed and came back seeing. John 9:7

Almighty God had the option to create a universe filled with people who look alike, i.e., exact replicas of one another. Can you imagine a world where all of us looked alike, where we couldn't tell one another apart because God designed all of us to be the same? Can you imagine a world where all of our passions and talents are the same? Fortunately, that was not what God has in mind.

God is too wise to be mistaken. In His own magnificent way, He created each one of us differently. I am confident of this—that God created each one of us for a unique purpose. Even when we cannot see His plan or when it seems like we cannot perceive His hand in our lives, my prayer is that every individual who has breath for another day will thank God for the grace given him/her to exist. We need to thank God for our individual lives and skills, and accept ourselves as we are, to allow God to use us to accomplish His purpose.

I recall a question the then President of the Presbyterian Church of Ghana National Ministers Conference put to me at the January 2015 Ministers' Conference held in Kwame Nkrumah University of Science and Technology, Kumasi. I had finished making a presentation at the conference on "Disability and God's family–the way forward." Having felt sorry for the actions and inactions of the church that had limited our inclusion and full participation in God's house, he went further, quizzing me about how the congregations that I had pastored accepted and dealt with me knowing that I had a disability. I told the Conference that the acceptance had been slow at the beginning, but in the middle of my stay in every station, I had been able to demonstrate to them that they should acknowledge God's strength that lies in disability.

I remember, on September 9, 2012, when I was having my send-off ceremony from one of the congregations in Accra, the then Senior Presbyter of that church remarked that "You have proved us wrong." I was not privy to events and discussions that had taken place prior to my arrival, but on that day, he revealed what had bothered their minds on my coming to pastor their congregation. But after some months, all their fears had melted away, and the church was seeing tremendous growth. One thing that fascinated him was my ability to stand and pray for hours and not get tired.

Thank God I was able to prove them wrong, though I didn't know I had to. I believe I was also able to change their general perception towards persons with disabilities, to let them know that we are different on purpose, and we need to acknowledge and complement the efforts and gifts of one other.

One of the fascinating thoughts for most people to accept is the fact that even from our mother's wombs, God chose everyone. God's blood flows through our veins. Regardless of the disability a person walks through life with, his/her role in God's plan is not wiped out. We are all children of God. We are all different on purpose, and that is what makes us worthy.

There are voices of defeat that will fill our minds with endless thoughts of guilt, but faith will require the courage to take a step, in whatever direction God gives us.

The amazing thing about Almighty God's creation is the fact that no other person in the world is made exactly like you and me. So irrespective of the narrative that society reinforces, you and I are original creations. So is the man and woman or little boy or girl whose plight is reduced to sitting on the corner of the street because he/she cannot see him/herself beyond the situation where he/she finds himself/herself.

At one point or another, you and I may have to fill the void for someone and remind him/her that God's love for him/her didn't fall short due to his/her circumstances. Nothing about our lives is a surprise to God. Just as no two people possess the same DNA, God has deposited a unique purpose in every single one of us.

I have come to depend fully on a God who can turn a dry patch into an oasis right in the middle of a desert, and make life bloom again when it has been abandoned. Through the lives of many men and women whose lives feel helpless, God still uses every one of us who can avail him/herself of Him to manifest his glory.

Not long ago, I was invited as a guest speaker at a retreat at Presbyterian Boys Senior High School, in Accra, Ghana. I was to speak on the theme "Abundant Grace." I spent many hours thinking it through and working to come up with an illustration to drum home my message. I wished I had the perfect words to share with the audience to convey that it was indeed impossible for God's perfection to create any of us as an imperfect reflection of Him. Even with our frailty and emotional and physical hurdles to overcome, God still rejoices in the fact that He has a destiny for each of us to fulfill and nothing that happens to us can derail that purpose.

I recalled the story of John Newton and his writing of the hymn "Amazing Grace." Newton was born in London in the early part of the eighteenth century, the son of the commander of a merchant ship which sailed the Mediterranean. At age of eleven John went to sea with his father and made six voyages with him before the elder Newton retired. John Newton ultimately became captain of his own ship, one which plied the slave trade.

Although he had had some early religious instruction from his mother, who had died when he was still a child, he had long since given up any religious convictions. However, in one of his voyages, when he had gone to bring slaves from Sierra Leone, the ship was caught in a turbulent storm on the high seas. At that moment, far away from what may have been God's plan for his life, he had the chance to share a thought that would live many years after his own death.

Newton remembered the God his mother had introduced him to earlier on in his life and prayed to Him. Miraculously, the cargo shifted to fill a hole in the ship's hull, and the vessel drifted to safety. Newton took this as a sign from the Almighty and marked that moment as his return to Christianity.

Later in his cabin, he reflected on what had happened and began to believe that God had addressed him through the storm and that grace had begun to work for him.

That is when he reflected and wrote the words;

> *Amazing grace! How sweet the sound*
> *That saved a wretch like me!*
> *I once was lost, but now am found;*
> *Was blind, but now I see.*
>
> *'Twas grace that taught my heart to fear,*
> *And grace my fears relieved;*
> *How precious did that grace appear*
> *The hour I first believed.*

Through many dangers, toils and snares,
I have already come;
'Tis grace hath brought me safe thus far,
And grace will lead me home.

The Lord has promis'd good to me,
His word my hope secures;
He will my shield and portion be,
As long as life endures.

Yes, when this flesh and heart shall fail,
And mortal life shall cease;
I shall possess, within the veil,
A life of joy and peace.

The earth shall soon dissolve like snow,
The sun forbear to shine;
But God, who call'd me here below,
Will be forever mine.

In Newton's state of powerlessness, when all hope had gone and he was faced with the danger of drowning, God miraculously intervened, and he, together with the crew, the slaves, and the cargo, was saved. Gradually, Newton began to respond to God's grace, and later in his life, became a preacher and a rector of St. Mary Woolnoth, in London. Newton acknowledged that it was grace that had brought him however far he had come. He could not have made it on his own.

I once read an inspirational story of a renowned man of God. It was just as moving as it was filled with incredible teaching moments for every one of us. It was a story that was a beautiful and humble testament to God's sufficient grace, even in our times of human weakness.

A man who had spent much of his adult life preaching the Word of God woke up from a hospital bed one day paralyzed. He had been abroad for medical treatment for an unrelated disease, and by the time he was to leave, part of his body—from his shoulders to the lower half of his body— had no feeling or moment. Nearly a month later, it looked as if his world had spun out of control. He believed in God's power to heal him instantly, but he was aware also of a God who knows how best to bring glory through our circumstances. Yet the questions rushed through his mind.

The therapies continued. He would spend almost a whole year in hospitals, hopping from one specialist to another. Perhaps just as easily as his condition had deteriorated, his life could turn around suddenly. Why not? He was a man filled with faith and served a God full of miracle-working power. He prayed and he kept on holding on to every faith he could muster. Nothing changed.

Years after this ordeal, the man held on to one promise he'd made to himself: that he would recover soon. He soon gained some movement in his right hand, and gradually partial mobility and sensitivity in some parts of his body. Through it all, he was convinced that Almighty God knew what was best for him, and was making him live through this reality for a purpose. Nothing in his life—not even the accident—had been for naught.

Life after life, story after story gives us a window into the heart of Almighty God, showing us that only He is able to use any one of us regardless of what our limitations seem to be. I have come to learn that in God's eyes, whatever He has called you and me to accomplish in this life is not beyond our physical or emotional capability to do. If only we can come to the point of submission to His will, we too can have our lives transformed and work again.

The purpose of our lives ought to hinge on the fact that the God who created the universe and every magnificent thing that lives in it did not create you and me as an afterthought. We are all indeed worthy in His eyes, and whatever the purpose for which we have been created, no event or setback will derail His perfect plan for every one of us.

Nick Vujicic was on stage in front of an audience who were utterly marveled at the joy in the heart of a man whose words were filled with much wisdom, as they were with laughter. Nick is an Australian Christian evangelist and a well-known inspirational speaker. His sermons are indeed inspiring, and perhaps it is because he doesn't take himself too seriously, and invites the audience to listen to his message without expecting any applause. Nick was born with a rare medical condition—tetra-amelia syndrome. He was born missing all four of his limbs.

I can only imagine what he must have endured as a child and adolescent. We can only imagine the frustrations he would have lived with as he saw other children and young boys running around in the rain and sun, and all he could do was to imagine what that must be like. It had to be tough. The miracle in his life is the fact that his parents didn't abandon him. Nick had been fortunate to have parents who did not need to consult any spiritual healers to determine what they had to do with their young son.

Vujicic wrote that he has always kept a pair of shoes in his closet because he believes a miracle will happen someday. While he waits on his miracle, he has been busy since his teenage years speaking to millions of people around the world to help others find joy and meaning in life.

Nick Vujicic's condition has not changed, but his understanding of God's abundant grace upon his life has inspired millions of people around the world. He went on to start the non-profit organization, Life Without Limbs, and through his story, perhaps sends a message of hope and reassurance to another who has convinced him/herself to feel downtrodden and worthless.

Unfortunately, there is absolutely nothing that instructs anyone in society to relate to you and me as we would prefer. There is also no label on anyone's forehead that tells their story to anyone they meet. Perhaps if that were the case, people would stop to read our life stories and share some empathy. There is a woman walking the streets of any city you can imagine with her back bent, and she struggles everywhere she turns. If only she could tell of the terrible plane crash she amazingly survived, maybe you and I would understand that she sees herself as a miracle, rather than wallowing in self-pity.

Maybe all of us should have the heart to hear the silent stories in the lives of the people we meet, and share in their journey. I am confident that we will make a difference in our societies, if we take the time to see another's obstacle as that of our own, and another's pain through a lens that may cause us to be just a little kind or thoughtful, rather than turn a blind eye to it.

I pray for the day when all of us will be more consumed about the heart of the people we meet along our journey, just as much as we pay attention to their outside. A day when we will truly find meaning in the fact that God in His infinite wisdom did not create us all in one way, as if we had just jumped off a wheel in an assembly line. God breathed life into each of us as a unique representation of Himself.

One of the most intriguing observations I made years ago was about the fashion industry and the walkway. The most intricate designs are embellished with every ornament imaginable to make the clothing exquisite. So it is in life. What people see is the familiar image of models dressed in a designer's creations, strutting down a walkway, with an audience looking on in admiration. The lights and camera and stage make them look even more enchanting.

All the attention is given to the appearance to make it as glamourous as could be imagined, but not a moment is spent caring about what that same person looks on the inside. In fact it doesn't matter because the fashion experts have found this interesting fact to be true, that humanity and society do not care about anything more than what we see on the outside.

Unfortunately, all of us are guilty at being expert judges at defining people's lives and futures based on how we see them. Rather than seeing a person as God's creature, full of life, full of hope and having a destiny, we tend to tie a person's worth to the clothing and shoes and the flawless walk on that walkway.

Then we hear stories about how some of the same models who were so mesmerizing in one instant feel so broken and sometimes even on the verge of committing suicide. In stories after stories we find that all the glitter and the promise of beautiful magazine pages does well to conceal a person's true state only for a moment. Sooner or later, they step out into the real world. We find that God is more concerned with our hearts and inner person than He is about our external appearance. In God's sight what defines a person is often what is unseen.

There is a story of a young American who was working on a routine day as an electrician, when a wiring failure changed his life and future suddenly. About 13,000 volts from a transformer went through his body in an instant. He was fortunate to survive the accident, but he was injured in many parts of his body, and both his arms had to be amputated because of the extensive damage to them.

It took years of rehabilitation to find his joy. The road to recovery must have been so weighty that I imagine there are days he would wish he had not been at work and touched the wires. He is working every day, finding new ways to live a fulfilling life, with his only hope being that surviving the accident gave him a chance to do the things he had not been able to do.

In Ghana and many parts of the world, children born with autism or any similar disability are immediately labelled *stupid*. *Autism*, the spectrum disorder that shows itself as challenges with social skills, repetitive behaviors, speech and nonverbal communication, has become prevalent in Ghanaian society. Just as researchers and medical professionals race against time to help make a difference in its occurrence, the plight of many children and families cannot be overlooked.

If the child is fortunate enough to escape the cultural confines and the often strange interpretations of his condition, walking through life in a society where he is an outcast becomes unbearable. He quickly latches on to the label. No matter the courage and focus, many young people struggle with any task from school work to other activities that most would consider routine. There is no telling how a person is doing his/her best to persevere to overcome his/her challenges. You and I have no ability to define what Almighty God is yet to do with the life of the person whose difference is all we see about him.

Disabilities like autism gradually emerged onto the forefront of social discussions in recent years. For much of the time, it was a taboo. It was a plight only the families had to endure, and they often hid their child in shame. Society had already concluded that the child was not good enough. In Ghana, the term *"gbiligbili"* was assigned, a derogatory slang to describe a person who is physically and mentally challenged. Rather than counting our blessings for not having to go through our day with the hurdle another has to endure, we stoop to ridicule and shame.

In different parts of the world, there is a nickname—usually a derogatory one—that fits their stereotype. Many children grow up sneering at and mocking the life of anyone with physical or other types of disabilites. Is it any surprise that we all grow up and unfortunately are desensitized to the plight of the person who stands next to us, but whose journey is much different from our own?

I have come to learn that life has a way of dealing with you and me, dealing us a hand that we could never have imagined. The frustration can be devastating for many people. Even through the downcast moments, it is important we manage to lift our heads up to remind ourselves that God indeed has a plan and a purpose for each one of us. His plans for our lives are not erased because of some challenge we have to live through, or because of a disability.

I learned, especially in the times when nothing in life seemed to be going my way, that God is still on the throne, and He alone has me in the palm of His hand. Because of this realization, I have been incredibly careful about my confessions in the moments when everything looks bleak, and I am helpless. Our confessions can bring depression and defeat to us, just as easily as they can become the launching pad to help us to stir our faith. None of this happens by itself. The reassuring truth is that we serve a God with all power in His Hands who can bring each and every one of us to an expected end.

Grace finds you and me just as we are and gives us the chance to live again. Grace takes our place when we feel we have lost it all, and gives us a second chance to start over. Grace meets us at the point of death and breathes a new life into us to make us stand again. That is an unmerited favor, and that is what grace is. Something we do not deserve, and we cannot even fathom the breadth of its worth.

The tragedy in all of humanity, and woven into all of us, is how we devalue grace. As it is with anything, the moment we give ourselves a reason to assign less value to something, whether consciously or otherwise, it loses its significance for you and me. The rather fascinating part of this entire story is that regardless of how much we trample upon grace, it never loses its worth. It never loses its power.

Jesus went ahead of you and me and made the sacrifice for us. This sacrifice became the bridge that connects us to Almighty God. Even in our deplorable state as human beings whose lives are nothing more than just a blur in a moment, Jesus cared enough for you and me to stand in the gap for us. That is grace. That is the power of grace.

If we are ever able to come to a moment when we truly appreciate the fact that left to our own, there is nothing we can accomplish or become, we are humbled. In that same vein, we recognize that we are created for a purpose and we are different on purpose. If we truly understand that there is nothing that protects us from some tragedy in the next second or even death in the next minute, we probably are slow to be impressed by our own works.

The beautiful part of my life is that despite my own challenges, God will let His will in my life come to fruition. He is still working in my life to bring me to an expected end. I have had to remind myself over and again, that for such a time as this, and for such a purpose as that which He has placed in my heart, God has fearfully and wonderfully made me, and that is the same for you.

The same injection that left me paralyzed could have killed me. And that is a piece of knowledge I have always held so dear and understood that truly, no matter what happens in my life, it is the unseen hand of God that has kept me safe and alive. It has been His grace, and no matter what challenges I have to live with physically, there is nothing that can ever leave a stain on my heart and hinder me from becoming all that Almighty God is calling me to do.

I thank God for the grace that He extends to us every single day, none of which we deserve.

I pray that this work edifies believers, strengthens our faith and brings assurance to everyone that

God inclines His ear to our heart's cry. Whatever story we go through and however many tears we shed, God's plan comes alive even through our joy and pain. In the same way, I'm encouraged that our physical temporal conditions don't define the rest of our lives.

I learned at some point in my Christian journey that it takes an encounter with Jesus to experience God and grace for ourselves. Once we have that, and are fortunate to have God break the shackles off our lives, we will learn to surrender our heart to His will. God's heart is devoid of prejudice. He never tramples on anyone, and regardless of what temporary obstacle they may have.

The sobering exhortation for us all is the fact that once you have experienced grace and understood the worth of Christ's sacrifice, it is not difficult to extend grace to another person. The sad truth is that, with every blessing, we become comfortable, and become complacent. We forget where God has brought us from, from darkness to see His light.

Grace sees us for who we were made to be, rather than who we are in the moment. Grace sees past our shortcomings and our challenges. Amazing grace sees beyond what society has rejected because it is unpopular or the norm. Grace finds every heart and every person whom Almighty God has created in His own image and reassures them that there is never a blemish that is so deep or so ugly that it separates them from Him. That is the amazing nature of God's grace.

That is what grace does—gently reminding us that all of us are created for a purpose, and made different on purpose.

CHAPTER 9

BEYOND THE GUILT

*Memories from Ogbomosho.
The Sight of Bartimaeus.*

⁸ The neighbors and those who had seen him before as a beggar said, "Is not this the man who used to sit and beg"? John 9:8.

Society may not know when its actions and inactions crush the heart of another, but the awareness for expressing genuine love and care towards a brother or sister should be a fruit of grace, not guilt. It is incredibly freeing to live with the perspective that life owes you nothing, and that there is nothing in life to which one is entitled. Every moment of our lives is a product of God's grace and mercy, and my prayer is that we will not live in a society where we create an uncomfortable atmosphere by pointing out every missed step or opportunity that someone thought they deserved.

In October 2010 in Ghana, the Ecumenical Disability Advocates Network (EDAN) of the World Council of Churches and the West African Association of Theological Institutions (WAATI), met to deliberate on disability issues, and how instructors should address these issues and teach at the seminaries and the universities in the region. Insightful presentations were made, and at the end of the workshop, there was a strong urge to continue and complete a curriculum.

Two of the participants from Nigeria, Rev. Professor Samuel Abiola, who was at the time President of the Nigeria Baptist Theological Seminary (NBTS), in Ogbomosho, and Professor Matthew Ojo, a New Testament scholar and lecturer at Obafemi Awolowo University (OAU), Ille-Ife Osun State, Nigeria, were charged to make the necessary preparations for the follow-up consultation to take place in the following year in Nigeria.

In 2011, I was part of the delegation leaving Accra to the Nigeria Baptist Theological Seminary, Ogbomosho, Oyo State. I was thrilled at the thought of seeing other cultures, even across the African continent. I left by Arik Air to Lagos, the commercial capital of Nigeria. I was on the same flight with a colleague of the EDAN. I called her Auntie Gerty. She was visually impaired.

At Murtala Muhammed Airport, Lagos, Nigeria, we met our host and also some guests who had arrived earlier from other African countries, and we were sent to the Nigeria Baptist Theological Seminary, in Ogbomosho, about a four-hour drive from Lagos.

The next morning I led the devotion and read from Mark's Gospel 10:46-52:

> *[46] Then they came to Jericho. As Jesus and his disciples, together with a large crowd, were leaving the city, a blind man, Bartimaeus (which means "son of Timaeus"), was sitting by the roadside begging.*
> *[47] When he heard that it was Jesus of Nazareth, he began to shout, "Jesus, Son of David, have mercy on me!"*

> *⁴⁸ Many rebuked him and told him to be quiet, but he shouted all the more, "Son of David, have mercy on me!"*
> *⁴⁹ Jesus stopped and said, "Call him."*
> *So they called to the blind man, "Cheer up! On your feet! He's calling you." ⁵⁰ Throwing his cloak aside, he jumped to his feet and came to Jesus.*
> *⁵¹ "What do you want me to do for you?" Jesus asked him. The blind man said, "Rabbi, I want to see."*
> *⁵² "Go," said Jesus, "your faith has healed you." Immediately he received his sight and followed Jesus along the road.*

I continued with the exposition. Bartimaeus meant the son of Timaeus, and his story had an intriguing tone to it. Timaeus came from the Greek word "timaios" which meant "highly prized." The name denotes "worthy" as well as "honor." But when Bartimaeus became blind, he turned a beggar. The man who had been born a son of honor was now living on the benevolence and charity of passers-by. What an unfortunate irony.

In the story, upon hearing that Jesus was passing by, Bartimaeus did what was not popular for a man of his reputation. He began to shout for help from Jesus. "Jesus, Son of David, have mercy on me!" he kept on shouting. This statement from Bartimaeus was a theological statement, calling Jesus "Son of David." This is a Christological title, indicating Jesus' Messiahship. By calling Jesus "Son of David," Bartimaeus affirmed that he (Jesus) was the Anointed One of God, set apart by God, to redeem all humankind and creation unto Himself. Though Bartimaeus was blind physically, spiritually and theologically, he was not unperceptive, for he knew who Jesus was, and the mission he was carrying. Given the space and time, persons with disabilities can contribute their share to theology and any issue at stake.

The rather intriguing part of the story was the revelation God deposited in the heart of a man whose eyes couldn't see what everyone else could see, but who saw something none of the people could see.

For God, it didn't matter that Bartimaeus was imperfect in the eyes of his society. Bartimaeus had heard enough about Jesus that he could believe in his power, although Bartimaeus himself had not seen Jesus perform any miracles.

We find also that while Bartimaeus was shouting to attract Jesus, his own people in the community asked him to shut up. But the more they urged him to keep quiet, the more he shouted. Bartimaeus became the lone ranger struggling to be heard by Jesus, when the people around with all their spiritual blinders carefully tucked in place, had concluded that Bartimaeus couldn't be worthy to catch Jesus' attention. It was the minority against the majority.

My encouragement to anyone who has a disability or is feeling the weight of one in one way or another is to be reassured that God's heart and eyes are not turned away from your pain and cries. Dreams that are trapped behind apparent challenges will not die, because the God who places dreams in the hearts of his children is faithful to bring them to life, if we will believe again. If a man/woman can find it in his/her heart to speak aloud again, just like Bartimaeus did, Jesus will stop for him/her.

I can imagine that if the people around Bartimaeus saw Jesus quite the way he (Jesus) did, they wouldn't have been so quick to urge him to shut up. Unfortunately, the world around us will not sit back for a voice that it expects to be silent, and let it drown out theirs. But God says keep speaking. Keep shouting. Many important dreams in life will not automatically come to light unless a person determines to allow God's grace to empower him/her to keep pushing ahead. Will it be uncomfortable sometimes? Certainly, it is. But when Bartimaeus persisted, he had his say and also had his way. He broke the norm of the community in which he lived.

Maybe if we were fully aware of the true impacts of our attitudes toward the man or woman who is blind or deaf or sitting in a wheelchair, we will pause for a second to examine our own hearts.

The marginalized and the lone voices in our societies will continue shouting, or advocating, even though the expectation will be to mute their voices instead.

I have found many scenarios where society struggles genuinely to understand the challenges of the situations they cannot fully comprehend, and where even well-meaning family members discourage and treat a person with disability with disdain. I have lived through moments when friends abandon and ridicule a person's dream with rebuttals like "building castles in the air," or "your hopes seem to be unachievable, even absurd."

In Ogbomosho, Nigeria, I had a chance to remind the people who had gathered that morning that just like Bartimaeus, the lesson rests in the fact that he never stopped shouting. For men and women who find themselves living in towns and villages where there is no proper attention paid to the plight of persons with disabilities, or where persons with disabilities are seen as objects and not subjects, sometimes all you are left with is your voice. Speak life. God has given every one of us a voice, and it is incredible how much of what we confess with our own mouths and believe in our hearts become our portion in life.

My prayer always has been not to apportion guilt, although our societies are too preoccupied with themselves to make another's challenge or need their priority. For the person whose plight has pushed them to the edges of society, my encouragement is in the reminder that you are there to shout, shout in your little corner. The world around you and me is listening.

I can vividly remember when I invited people to travel with me into worlds that on the surface may have looked very similar to their own, but they didn't stop long enough to pay attention. In every city and town, our communities build modern and public facilities and completely forget some of the most basic provisions to accommodate people whose disabilities make even the most routine task to you and me, a miracle. It is rather unfortunate to find that there is not even access to some of the facilities intended to attract persons with disabilities. In many cases, such access is added as a design afterthought.

In my own journey as a minister, I found it pretty disheartening to get to a place of worship and find that there is not even a simple ramp to enable people who can't climb steep staircases to make it into the facility.

I sigh at a striking example where a church facility that seemed to have made accommodations for persons with disabilities had access ways that only led to the main auditorium. There was no access to the altar and the pulpit, as if to make a statement that people with physical disabilities wouldn't have any reason to get closer to those sections.

While I explained the story of Bartimaeus, I remember looking into the crowd and seeing expressions of apparent guilt. It was as if they hadn't done enough when they could have. Jesus did not let the crowd dictate to him, for he heard the cry of Bartimaeus, the marginalized, and stopped for him. He sent the same people who were obstructing Bartimaeus from coming to him, to bring him closer. I can only imagine the guilt in their hearts. They meant to shut him up, as if they had been conditioned to do so. The more he shouted, the more they shut him up. But he persevered.

The environment, the culture, the society, and even the family may reject the calling from the heart, but I am excited to have a friend in Jesus who is indeed a friend to the poor and the destitute. I am thrilled to know of a Jesus who would never be too busy for a blind Bartimaeus.

In the midst of the multitude, the Lord still hears the cry of the oppressed and the abandoned. What seems pathetic in the life of Bartimaeus is not his physical blindness, but his own people who "disabled" him from connecting to Jesus. The disabilities we see in people's lives are not the impairments or the handicaps that have come about due to their individual medical conditions. Rather it is the disabilities from other people, the society, and cultures, sadly, even the churches, placed in the way as limitations. I am confident that if these limitations and restrictions are dealt with, persons with disabilities will throw away their "cloaks" that have confined them to the corners of life.

One thing I was incredibly impressed about in Bartimaeus' story was that when he was given the privilege to request from Jesus what he wanted him to do, he went straight to the point, and said: "Rabbi, I want to see." Unlike the man at the Pool of Bethesda, who complained a lot when Jesus moved in to heal him, Bartimaeus was simplistic and clear; he wanted to see. Bartimaeus, though blind, saw the power of sight and enlightenment resident in Jesus.

Jesus, the Son of David, is the Anointed One to give sight and enlightenment, not only to Bartimaeus, but to all creation. What I have come to find is that the world is filled with enough noise that if we are not careful, we will breeze through life without stopping for a moment to tune our ears to the weeping in our respective societies. No matter the frustration, I only pray that our faith and strength will not wane, but be encouraged to hear the cry and the shouts of the Bautimaeuses around us.

After my exhortation, a solemn quietness took over the room. Everyone seemed frozen in their seats. No one moved. While I delivered the message, the immediate feedback from the participants told a story of its own. I was unsure of what their response would be. My closing statement was met with a loud "Amen," and long applause.

When I took my seat, Rev. Professor Samuel Abiola who was serving as the President of the Seminary at the time, walked across to where I sat with a few of my colleagues. Professor Samuel Abiola said he had drawn some lessons from my devotion, but it was what he said next that I found particularly salient. He said he felt guilty. Then there was a slightly awkward silence as he tried to collect his thoughts.

Professor Abiola explained the source of his guilt, that he had been in a position where he could improve the reality of people with disabilities, but it never occurred to him to do so. He thought he had overlooked some of the simplest things that could have made a huge difference in someone's life. He had walked around hundreds of blind Bautimaeuses, and missed the chance to hear their cry.

Politely, I tried to assure him that guilt was not the emotion my teaching hoped to elicit. We both smiled. Professor Samuel Abiola thought he needed to apologize to the people with disabilities at the conference, hoping that his genuine epiphany would travel with us to different communities.

In his own world, as the president of the seminary, he had the opportunity to meet with some of his students who happened to have some form of disabilities, but it never occurred to him to make the campus truly disability-friendly. He admitted how it was not until a few days before the conference that they started feverishly constructing ramps at some vantage points of the school. The international nature of the conference compelled them to do this and felt it had taken him such a long time to effect such a simple change. He knew the plight of his own students, but he couldn't fully grasp their quiet challenges. Professor Abiola was almost in tears.

As he spoke, Professor Abiola felt the burden of the persons with disabilities, having organized the conference in a place where some people had to go to great lengths to attend. There, people using wheelchairs and crutches found it particularly difficult to climb the stairs. Some had to be carried upstairs, and it had not been a pleasant situation.

One of the most striking annotations he made of his own work had been the fact that the seminary had hurriedly built an accommodation facility to help the persons with disabilities who had come from outside, to make us feel comfortable. Oddly, the floor had been constructed with tiles and remained very slippery. That was evidence in itself that the seminary hadn't given much thought to the plight of the individuals who walked through their hallways and on their campus.

In Ogbomosho, Professor Abiola spoke towards the end of the morning session. As if the conference room had turned to a courtroom, Professor Abiola declared that he was guilty of not doing much to remove the limitations placed in the way of persons with disabilities. Another participant stood up and said he was also guilty. Soon, the ripples of Professor Abiola's "guilt" turned contagious enough to change the tone of the entire meeting. There was much more everyone could do in his or her own little way, and perhaps together we would make a difference in the lives of many young men and women in our communities.

One striking statement which to me was positive and served also as feedback came from Prof. Ogoromi, one of the Lecturers at Nigerian Baptist Theological Seminary: "I am going back to teach the Bartimaeus story again." Take it as guilt or a new revelation, she had gained a new insight into something she had taught for years—the story of Bartimaeus. I was humbled by the Professor's U-turn, going back to correct the wrongs. But I asked myself, "Where is she going to get all the students who have passed through her classes"? I knew it wasn't going to be possible, but at least she would carry a new perspective to teach her new students and anyone else she came across.

Bautimaeus' plight was no different from that of a young man who shared his story in one of the sessions of the Ogbomosho Consultation. It was tearful to hear of the stories of frustrations and disappointments that he had to endure to have a normal life. Samuelson was pursuing a Master's Degree at Obafemi Awolowo University, Ille-Ife, Osun State, Nigeria. Samuelson had been an energetic Christian student leader, who was working his best to combine his studies with God's work.

At the end of the third year, during the long vacation, the Christian students organized an outreach programme, going to evangelize in the villages to lead the people to Christ. On their way, they had an accident, which dealt a big blow to these young and energetic students who were on "fire" for the Lord. Samuelson got paralyzed in the aftermath, and could do nothing on his own. His dream of graduating the following year was on the verge of becoming a mirage. But for the strong will of Linda, Samuelson's fiancée, Samuelson's education would have suffered an abrupt end.

Samuelson had been confined to a wheelchair, but despite this, it was Linda who spent time training him how to use it. He had been so downhearted that he thought the world had come to an end for him. In fact he had decided not to continue his university education, his reason being that he would not be able to surmount the challenges he would face on campus as a person with a disability. When he had lost all hope and did not know what to do with his life, Linda told him, "Samuelson, you are going back to campus to complete your programme." Samuelson did not take it easy at all, and resisted. But Linda persisted, and encouraged him not to be discouraged so easily. Samuelson finally agreed. He did not have it easy at all; from the hall of residence to the lecture theatres, Samuelson met a lot of insurmountable limitations. But Linda was around to encourage him.

The most touching part of his testimony was when he told us that he could not attend a particular lecture for one of the New Testament Courses, because the lecture theatre was on the upper floor, and the building had no lift. When it was lecture time, Samuelson would be wheeled to the academic block and wait downstairs for his colleagues to come out from the lecture, and would borrow their lecture notes and copy them.

At the end of semester exam, Samuelson topped the class, to the surprise of everybody. The following semester, the lecturer wanted to see the person who had emerged first in his course, and he was told it was Samuelson who had never set foot at his lecture because he had a disability and could not climb upstairs. Prof. Matthew Ojo was surprised at the treatment Samuelson had to go through, for it was unknown to him. On the other hand, he became very sorry and he imagined there could have been others who may have been turned away inadvertently. Samuelson's story was a chilling account of the reality that many people like him had to endure, and one that was sobering to the core.

That semester, Prof. Matthew decided that his lecture was no longer going to take place upstairs; he brought the venue downstairs to include

Samuelson in his class, who had become more of a friend than a student to him. Prof. Matthew then took special interest in Samuelson, which encouraged him. Samuelson later married Linda, and was very grateful to her. When he concluded his story, some of us shed tears of joy. Personally, I was happy to see Samuelson leading a revitalized life, going back to continue his education to add value to himself. In May, 2017, I decided to check on him, and lo and behold, he had gotten his Ph.D. and was lecturing at Obafemi Awolowo University. Here is an excerpt from a letter he sent me:

> *Dear Rev. Ankomah,*
> *…I have finished my program but I am still in the department. My wife is also fine. God gave us a set of twins (a boy and a girl) last year February after over 17 years of marriage. We give glory to His holy name . . .*
> Samuelson Olufemi Kanayo (Ph.D.),
> Old Testament Studies & African Culture,
> Department of Religious Studies, Obafemi Awolowo University,
> Ile-Ife, 220005 Osun State, Nigeria.

When I received this letter, I was very happy for my brother in Christ, and more so for Linda, for I said, "God rewards faithfulness." The God we serve cannot be completely understood and there will remain some questions on our minds till we meet Him face-to-face. So in spite of this, we are encouraged by John Henry Newman's hymn, "Lead Kindly Light" of which a portion of the first stanza says. "Keep Thou my feet;

> *I do not ask to see*
> *The distant scene;*
> *One step enough for me."*

The relationship between Samuelson and Linda hadn't been without difficulties, but they trusted their God every moment and were never thrown into despair. They seemed to sing this hymn, acknowledging the sovereignty of God over their lives, humming, "Keep thou my feet . . . one step enough for me."

The lesson for everyone in Ogbomosho had not been about guilt or innocence. Rather, it had been about the grace to see the tears in our brother's and sister's eyes.

Someday we would all look back at what chances we had to change another person's day that we let slip by. We would look back someday and see where we could have made a difference but had not done enough to bridge the huge gap between persons with disabilities and the rest of the people in our communities. Someday we would look back to imagine how we missed the obvious opportunity in most of our schools to make them accessible to the disabled. We would look back and wonder how we missed the difficult lives that parents and caregivers had to endure when in many cases they were forced to relocate to new regions and towns, to have their child or loved one educated or cared for. It is particularly heartbreaking to hear of situations where mothers and fathers give up on their children with some form of disability because it becomes a burden too heavy for them to bear.

Unfortunately our society has turned into one where the fittest survives, and we would rather leave the next person behind if his story is unlike ours.

My prayer is that we will not respond to the issue of disability out of the guilt of not standing side by side with our brothers and sisters, or not having our ear tuned to their plight and cries when we can. Rather, we can begin today and take a bold step of doing the best we can to uplift and build. We do so, not because of duty or obligation, but because everyone is indeed worthy.

CHAPTER

10

AN AWAKENING

*Time for the Blind Man to Rise Up
and Walk to the Pool.*

⁵As long as I am in the world, I am the light of the world." John 9:5

As I went through my years in seminary, there were two questions in two different encounters that left a remarkable imprint on my mind. The first was Jesus as he first met Bartimaeus. The man had screamed to get Jesus' attention and done all he could even when the men told him to be silent.

Now he stood in front of Jesus.

*⁵¹Jesus asked, "What do you want me to do for you?"
The blind man answered, "Master, I want to see!"*

> *⁵²Jesus told him, "You may go. Your eyes are healed because of your faith."*
>
> Mark 10:51-52.

The second was another encounter at the Pool of Bethesda, also known as the Sheep Gate when Jesus met the man who had been sick for many years. He had been sick for so long that he probably was convinced this would be how he would have to spend the rest of his life.

Then he met Jesus,-

> *⁶When Jesus saw him lying there, and knew that he already had been in that condition a long time, He said to him, "Do you want to be made well?"*
> *⁷The sick man answered Him, "Sir, I have no man to put me into the pool when the water is stirred up; but while I am coming, another steps down before me."*
> *⁸Jesus said to him, "Rise, take up your bed and walk." ⁹And immediately the man was made well, took up his bed, and walked.*
>
> John 5:6-9.

These are two different scenarios, in each of which Jesus had to ask a simple question. Jesus was aware of the fact that it was entirely possible to have people who have lived with a challenge or hurdle, not only a disability, and become comfortable with their situation. Somehow the fact that their eyes can't see or their limbs cannot move as quickly as they wish has forced them to assume that their lives ought to travel along a certain trajectory. Jesus asked the men about what they wanted. If they weren't interested in the miracle, the bible perhaps would have recorded a different ending to the stories.

I was driving through a busy main road in Accra when the traffic light turned red and brought every one of the motorists to a screeching halt. It felt as if it was taking forever to change to green. I looked around and observed. Hawkers and street vendors rushed to the cars, in an effort to sell every fruit and craft they carried on their heads. They did not want to go home with any of the items they had carried to the roadside to sell.

A young man showed up suddenly from nowhere. He stood next to my car. He sold handkerchiefs. He seemed to be in a hurry, as another driver had beckoned him to buy one of his handkerchiefs. He was a man who had lost the strength in both of his lower limbs, and could not walk.

I did not know his story, but I imagined he had pushed hard to find the courage to be where he sat. He sat on a little wooden crate that had four wheels underneath, and with that, he sped from one car to another. He pushed himself and used his left hand to direct the wheels in the direction he wanted them to go. This whole time, the young man had the tray of handkerchiefs—there must have been several hundred of them—upright on his head.

I was fascinated watching the man go back and forth, each time looking around to see if another customer called for his attention. Soon the light would change from red to green, and he would have to wait on the side of the street until the red light came on again, and then, I imagined, he would do the same thing over again.

In the distance, another man stood quietly in the corner. He appeared to have some deformity in his left hand. It was wrapped in a sling, yet he moved it up and down where he stood without much care for any pain or discomfort. He too had been standing in the scorching sun for hours, but he was scrambling to find motorists who would see how pitiful he was. He would share his sob story, and wait for sympathy coins to drop into his small plastic bowl. He begged for anything he could get, standing next to the man who was weaving through cars to ply his trade.

The two images were equally striking. It was a powerful painting of two individuals who on the surface had some form of physical limitation and challenge, yet had taken completely different routes to live their lives. They were both looking for whatever opportunity came along, but one had convinced himself he didn't want to be a victim of a sob story or a charity case. One was living every day expecting a turnaround, and for his life story, that was still unfolding, to count. The other seemed to have resigned himself to the fact that his condition had permanently incapacitated his hand, and even his drive to pursue a fulfilling life. What he had once hoped for didn't matter to him anymore.

One of the most powerful truths, often left unsaid is the fact that every man or woman, no matter his/her physical, mental or emotional hurdle, is fearfully and wonderfully made in the image of Almighty God. God's eyes remain on every one of us to bring glory through us into the world. Nothing in our lives catches God by surprise. For men and women who will choose to arise in spite of the discomfort, a world finds a shining light in a God who uses every one of our circumstances, regardless of how uncomfortable they may appear, for a purpose we may very well never fully understand.

The young man who sat on the wooden crate had dared to rise up and see the transforming power of Christ's amazing grace in his routine life.

I am so grateful that we serve a God who has always been in the business of restoring lives, even the ones that society has condemned to their graves. He is calling every one of His children to an awakening, to rid ourselves of the excuse of not being good enough, simply because society has taught us to believe this for so long. God is calling you and me to shed the images of ourselves that tell us we are not whole, and unworthy. God is asking you and me to refrain from allowing society's definition of our identity to shape our destiny.

> *The hand of the Lord was on me, and he brought me out by the Spirit of the Lord and set me in the middle of a valley; it was full of bones. ² He led me back and forth among them, and I saw a great many bones on the floor of the valley, bones*

> *that were very dry. ³ He asked me, "Son of man, can these bones live?"*
>
> Ezekiel 37:1-3

He alone can let dry bones live again, and can bring life and freshness into dead situations. Society may see you as "useless" or "good for nothing," but God sees you to be vessels that have His encapsulated power residing in you. It is worth stating, as obvious as it may seem, that the only thing the world can see about any person is what is outward. The world around us, with all its perfection, sees nothing about the heart of a person. Only God can. Only He has all the power to make dry bones breathe again, and rise from what once was impossible. Even when a person seems to have been crushed by dejection and challenges from his/her emotional and physical handicap, there is no situation so overwhelming that God writes a person off.

God's grace and goodness are unending, and are enough for the dead and dry bones in all of our lives to live again. What the world may see as unsalvageable, God sees His son and daughter who ought to rise up and choose to live again, salvaged.

For every man or woman, boy or girl whose life has changed from what it could have become because of an illness, an impairment or a challenge, my prayer and words of encouragement to such a person are that he/she is worthy. God did not make any mistakes when he formed you and me in His image and with a perfect will for our lives.

I remember a song we sang in my local church when I was a young boy. *"Sɛnea mete biara meyi me Nyame n'ayɛ"*, translated to mean that irrespective of my circumstance or seemingly imperfect situation, I will praise my God. My encouragement for people who find themselves in the minority and even in the margins of society, is to latch onto the unfailing grace of God that restores and refines.

The call is to rise up. I am confident of this, that through Almighty God's abundant mercies no situation is so debilitating that we cannot fulfill the path God has called us to walk. Being alive in this moment in history is a testimony to the plans God still has for every one of His children.

Anytime I walk across a major street in Accra, I cannot help but see the discouraging sights of men and women who have given up on themselves, and convinced themselves that they will spend the rest of their lives as burdens to society. Some of them may have even admitted that their lives will be forever seen as imperfect to others, and that their stories end as worthless.

The unfortunate storylines are ones that men and women, when confronted with a host of emotional or physical hurdles, many of which they couldn't have avoided, turn to alcohol to numb their pain. I have heard countless stories of people whose challenges may have happened to them at birth, and many more through some unfortunate accident, but sadly seek to find some relief at the bottom of a liquor bottle and in the comfort of drugs.

It is my hope that beyond the physical manifestation of miracles, as God wills for each of our lives, that the blind should hope to live again, rather than stand on the fringes of life and wonder what life they could have had. Yes, society and government institutions will have to create meaningful social programs to achieve a lasting impact, but what good will a program be, if persons with disabilities have given up on themselves even before they begin?

Yes, the challenges may be a bit daunting and perhaps more than those of the next person, but the fact of life will remain that none of us is perfect, and everyone has a challenge of his/her own. The amazing part of each of our stories is that with God's help, the dry bones in our lives get the chance to live again and see the purpose for which we have been created.

For mothers and fathers who have accepted their lives as destitute and hopeless, the challenge will be for all of us to encourage them to arise from their despair in order to live in the fullness of the life Almighty

God called them to. The corners of the street should not be their final destination. Living a life of dejection and hopelessness should not be the destiny of men and women to whom God's grace is sufficient.

The transforming power of Jesus' blood still changes lives. The time is now, for the blind, the hard hearing, and every person with any disability to rise up in his/her heart and live again. God breathed the breath of life into us and each person's life is perfect, because God's divine breath is flowing through every one of us.

We are all worthy, and that includes the man or woman who has spent years stuck in a depression because of his/her physical condition. Without Christ's hope, we will be without any helper to guide our next steps. I am a living testimony to the certainty that God can indeed give us the grace to see our dreams come alive if we come to embrace the truth that "we can do all things through Christ who strengthens us." The uplifting reminder to everyone who lives with or who is in the life of someone with a disability should be, not to allow the present situation to define what becomes of the rest of his/her life.

Whenever I have had the opportunity to encourage people in communities and also in churches, I have often asked that we determine to rise up in our hearts, as that is where the work begins. Once we take the first bold step, no matter the challenges in our lives, we can afford to trust God's unfailing hand to bring the right people to our lives who will become the specific helping hands we need to help carry on with our purpose. We get awakened when we embrace God's provision for our lives. Our societies get awakened when we see the boy or girl or man or woman, not as a stranger, but as a person towards whom we should feel obligated, to encourage them to live their most fulfilling life.

My prayer is that a person with a disability be reminded that even though he or she may be blind or visually impaired, he/she is not helpless. A person may be hard of hearing, but that is not a reason to define him/her as hopeless. Every one of us is worthy, and God does not expect anything less.

On one Thursday, 14 June 2018, after we had closed from a mid-morning prayer meeting, held in my church every Thursday from 9:00 A.M. to 11:00 A.M., Alex, a security personnel and a member of my church, approached me to tell me some good news about his marriage. He and his wife had gotten married in October 2016, and a whole year passed with no sign of pregnancy. I approached them, counseled them and prayed with them. They were very appreciative of this, and that encouraged me and the entire church to continue praying with them.

On this particular Thursday morning, Alex came to tell me that when his wife visited the hospital, her doctor told her she was two months pregnant. I was very delighted and felt happy for them. I gave thanks to God for using me to bring a miracle into their lives. This is just one of the instances of how God is using me to affect lives positively for Him. Persons with disabilities can also give back to their societies to better the lot of numerous lives. I say this with all humility. We can also say with Peter, "Silver or gold I do not have, *but what I have I give you . . .*" Acts 3:6 (emphasis mine).

There is a lot of potential locked up in you, so do not write yourself off, for God your maker is waiting for your contribution to help empower the dejected, the unemployed, the sick, the depressed, the unsaved, etc. You can make a great impact on your generation and beyond. Stand up and be counted.

That same afternoon, I visited Ayoo Photo Studio at Alajo, a small town in Ghana's capital city, Accra. The manager of this studio, Andrews K. Mensah, known in the neighborhood by the nickname Ayoo, is a person with walking disability, though he is not confined to the use of crutches or a wheelchair. Ayoo was born without a disability, but at the age of nine, after a short protracted illness, he was given an injection which resulted in the twisting of both his legs.

This affected his schooling, but God being so good, he was able to get on his feet again, using his right arm to support his right leg when he moved. This had affected the curvature of his body, but Ayoo did not let his disability relegate him to the backstage. Born a talented drummer, Ayoo was all over the place playing for various bands, and prominent among them was Senior Eddie Donkor's "Asiko Train Band."

In 1992, Ayoo became born again, and he stopped playing for secular bands, and directed all his energy and drumming expertise to perform in God's house. Ayoo is still playing drums at church, and also mentors up and coming drummers, impacting greatly on lives as a musician. Having learnt photography from his father in his childhood, at Asamankese, in the Eastern Region of Ghana, where he was helping his father develop negatives in the studio's darkroom, Ayoo decided to set up his own photo studio when he moved to Alajo.

He told me of his struggle in the early part of his life, where some members of his family had disdained him, considering him as not worthy, all due to his disability. This unfriendly relationship made him unhappy living among his relatives, and compelled him to leave home very early in life to seek solace elsewhere. This brought him to Accra to come and live on his own. As a strong-willed person, Ayoo was determined to succeed and to send a message to persons who automatically write off persons with disabilities as good for nothing. Among his siblings, Ayoo was the only one who took their father's profession to a higher level, a feat that amazed the father himself. With more than thirty years' experience in the photography industry, Ayoo had trained close to ten people, who today are plying their trade in their respective places.

My first encounter with Ayoo was around the year 2012, when I set eyes on him at Word Miracle Church (now Perez Chapel International) headquarters, at Dzorwulu, Accra. It was an induction service for the Director of GHACOE Women's Ministry, Mrs. Ofori Lartey. There, Ayoo was the official photographer to the General Overseer of the Perez Chapel Int., Bishop Charles Agyin Asare, and was covering the service. Was it a paradox to see a person with a walking disability being the official photographer for a miracle worker? It may sound odd, but one should not lose sight of the fact that it is God who heals and not human beings.

In a recent interaction, Ayoo told me that it was a service he decided to render to the man of God, and he did it for two years. I was inspired by that statement and wondered what had become of society's voluntary spirit, emanated from Christ. "For even the Son of Man did not come to be served, *but to serve*, and to give his life as a ransom for many" (emphasis mine) Mark 10:45. Let us persevere to serve and give back to our society and country, irrespective of disability or otherwise. In short, Ayoo was contributing his quota to the growth and survival of the economy and God's kingdom. He was giving back to society, and was full of praise to God.

Ayoo has remained a source of inspiration to a lot of people in Alajo's vicinity and beyond. Every person with a disability has some potential locked up in him/her, and must employ every technique to unearth that potential to contribute to society. What can you do for your society? You can make it and make a difference.

There are no mountains of challenges ahead in our lives so tall that prayer and grace cannot sustain us to climb over them. But we have to rise up and determine to climb. There is no ocean of obstacles so wide that the grace of God cannot help us to sail across. Rather than sit on the sidelines of life and condemn our future, we can take one step of faith after another. I am confident that with every step, we ask God through our actions to intercede on our behalf where we may not be able to go on our own. God will light our paths and lift us up whenever our strength is insufficient to move on our own.

In our churches and communities, after we've prayed all we can, God is asking us to rise up and do the work. I can imagine that there may be some people whose "rise up" moment will be going back to school and pursuing a vocation. The bold step of faith may very well be following a dream that you have thought of over and again, but which you haven't found the courage to act upon. It could be learning a trade, or doing whatever God inspired your heart to do.

Indeed God's miracle-working power is still at work in the world, but God will not do anything you and I can and should do on our own. It is convenient to do nothing, and say it's "in God's hands." If anything, the Christian should be setting an example for the world to follow, rising up in faith where society says we are too crushed and 'crippled' to go. We should count on God's unfailing grace to give us the strength to pursue our dreams and hopes when society doesn't expect anything from us.

In writing about his plight, the apostle Paul reasoned that his own thorn in the flesh may very well have been God's way of keeping him from becoming conceited.

> *"I was given a thorn in my flesh, a messenger of Satan, to torment me.*
> *⁸ Three times I pleaded with the Lord to take it away from me.*
> *⁹ But he said to me, "My grace is sufficient for you, for my power is made perfect in weakness." Therefore I will boast all the more gladly about my weaknesses, so that Christ's power may rest on me.*
> *¹⁰ That is why, for Christ's sake, I delight in weaknesses, in insults, in hardships, in persecutions, in difficulties. For when I am weak, then I am strong.*
> 2 Corinthians 12:7-10.

It was with this powerful declaration that the apostle Paul set out to change the world, in spite of his own limitation. Even in the face of his most significant accomplishments, he understood the power of Almighty God that makes everything we are and everything we do worthy, even in our weakness.

From the story of Jesus meeting the man who had been born blind, I found how the people in that era easily absorbed the negative attitudes that were acceptable regarding persons with disabilities. It was particularly remarkable to see how religious leaders seemed more concerned about the Sabbath ritual than its significance to a person who came to participate.

It is no surprise that Bartimaeus was ordered to be silent when he screamed to get Jesus' attention. It was no coincidence that a man had sat next to a pool for several years but could not find one person to take the focus off himself for a moment, to help him get a miracle. It was no coincidence that that congenitally blind man was viewed by everyone—including Jesus' disciples—as a hindrance to their religious experience.

As uncomfortable as it may be to think about, even before we exercise our faith, every one of us will have a choice to make. We have to choose whether life's circumstances will immobilize us, or if we can turn our hearts to God's grace and take our next step of faith. In my own humble journey, I can be a testimony to the fact that it is not the easiest to do, and often, we may never be able to move. But that is where God's grace kicks in, when our strength alone cannot carry us to our next stop.

I have learned that there is indeed no situation in our lives that is beyond His ability to resolve. We serve a prayer answering God, and I am confident of this, that if a society can turn our hearts to see one another through the lens of Almighty God, we will see our lives transformed into what He has called each and every one to become.

God is asking every man and woman, regardless of his/her own challenge, to be ready to rise up and scream to get his attention. The tragedy is that often, society's satisfaction in what the majority finds comfortable drowns the voice of the man or woman who seeks the God who transforms lives.

CHAPTER

11

WORTHY

*God's Plan for our Lives are
not Erased with a Disability*

[20] *"We know he is our son," the parents answered, "and we know he was born blind. 21 But how he can see now, or who opened his eyes, we don't know. Ask him. He is of age; he will speak for himself."* John 9: 20-21

It is amazing how refreshing life gets when we get to be honest with ourselves and live each waking moment knowing that it is only God who is capable of filling us with His strength to make it through the day. On our own, our imperfections are enough to let our bodies fall apart any moment, and anyone is just one unfortunate incident away from a dramatic life change. When we have the humility to accept the truth of our imperfections, our vulnerabilities don't drive a wedge between who we are and the person God has destined us to become.

One thing I have come to know is that God has enough grace for every weakness and He alone can mould us into becoming who He wants us to be. The good news is, no matter where we are in life, with all our scars and frustrations, our vulnerabilities and insecurities, He calls us worthy.

I recall a time in December 2010, when I had been newly stationed as pastor at the Resurrection Congregation of the Presbyterian Church of Ghana, Accra-Central. Sisi, my beloved mother, was to come over to visit and spend Christmas with my family. My joy of pastoring one of the biggest congregations in the Presbyterian Church of Ghana was short-lived, as my focus shifted to care for Sisi. She had a sudden stroke while making a stopover at Jane's, my eldest sibling's place at Ashale Botwe, a suburb of Accra. We took her back to Okorase-Koforidua for treatment. We tried everything we could, and spoke to all the doctors we could find in our desperate efforts to get Sisi back on her feet again. She didn't get well.

On New Year's Day 2011, my mother passed on to eternal glory. The woman that I remember as having been there for me my whole life was gone. I thought back to when she had to help prop me up, and had to help her son cope with the hostile environment he found himself in as a person with disability. I spent most of my childhood days on my mother's back, as she tirelessly carried me to wherever she went or I needed to be.

The memory I hung on to, more than any other, was of sitting back patiently to hear my mother recount what she found to be the one of the most difficult moments of her entire life. I can still remember her eyes moisten with tears, but she did everything she could to keep her face bright with a smile. I was the last of four children, and I can imagine the joy in a mother's heart when I arrived on that calm September night. Through my toddler years, I grew up healthy like any other boy would.

There was certainly nothing out of the ordinary. I was about one year old when I began taking my first steps and running carelessly everywhere I could, and doing my best to climb anything I could find. At age two, my mother and I were planning to travel up north to visit my father, who had been posted to Tanchara-Kunyukuo, in the Lawra District in a teaching position. Making a journey at that time from the southern part of the country to the northern part was very strenuous, as the roads were in deplorable condition. The winding roads were untarred and the random bumps soon became a routine part of the journey. It was going to take us about three full days to travel from Koforidua to Tanchara-Kunyukuo, a journey of about six-hundred kilometers. Kumasi, the second biggest city in Ghana, had been and still is the linking city between the north and the south.

We were planning to stop briefly in Kumasi, but my mother noticed I didn't look too well. I had fallen sick and my body temperature was gradually becoming a concern for my mother. She thought it would be best to send me to a hospital in Kumasi, after which we would continue our journey north. The details of her conversations with the doctors and nurses seemed hazy as she tried her best to recollect anything from that time.

The nurses gave me an injection to cure the fever. Unfortunately, whatever medicine they injected me with, made me crumple to the floor, and I could not walk again. I lost control of any ability to use my legs, and my parents had to spend the rest of their time battling with the reality of raising a child with a disability. It would become the most frustrating time of my parents' life and they did all they could to retrace the moment where all suddenly turned gloomy. Nothing helped.

My parents wouldn't accept that it was my lot in life, so they were determined to turn back the hands of time to that afternoon before we walked into the hospital. From that day, they would try everything and listen to anyone to help me walk again, but nothing seemed to work. They would not give up. My parents would send me from one hospital to another, one herbalist to another, and one prayer camp to another. Though they didn't get an immediate solution to my problem, they were not worried, and never gave up on me. I imagine their hearts must have been heavy with uncertainty.

One thing that I can never forget, though, was the dignity with which my parents treated me, and how they never missed an opportunity to show me all the love a parent could show to his/her child. It made the greatest impression on my heart and in my life, because with every smile, they reminded me that I was indeed, worthy.

One day, help came from above. My mother told me that, one afternoon in a quiet sleep, she had a dream of a man in a white robe giving her a walking stick. That dream marked a turning point in my life. After that dream, my mother decided to take a leap of faith and got me a walking stick. My mother, who could not have thought of this in her wildest imaginings, was teaching me how to use a stick to walk. I was barely five years old. A dream was coming true, as with the help of the stick, I could slowly stand up on my feet again. It took a long time, but little by little, my mother guided me.

I can imagine the smile on my parents' faces, knowing that somehow they had given me a second chance at moving around again. It would never be the same as for any of the other boys, but my parents also had to learn the incredibly difficult lesson that my journey and destiny was to be different. Though I still needed care as a child with a disability, the burden of always being carried about at my mother's back was reduced, unless it was for long distances.

At age six, I started school at Okorase Local Authority Methodist Primary School. Even though I had started walking with a stick, there was very little I could do by myself. I still needed support from others. The distance from Sakyibea, the village where we lived, to Okorase where the school was situated, was about three kilometres. It was impossible for me to commute to school, and in many cases in the country, that would be the end of education for a child with a disability. My story didn't end there.

Chapter 11: Worthy

My mother would carry me to school on her back, and be happily waiting outside for me at the end of the day to pick me up and take me home. Later, my uncle Kofi Panin, who was a senior in the same school, became the person who would carry me to school and make sure I was back home safely. In a community where they could have easily given up on a young boy, which probably would have been understandable by many, they were determined to not give up on me.

Soon my two elder brothers, William and Samuel, and my cousin, Kofi Kissiedu were also taking turns in carrying me every day. It is quite unfortunate that Kissiedu and William were called to eternal glory in 2015 and 2017 respectively. I recall writing and reading the siblings' tribute to our late brother, William Acquaah Cromwell. With boundless gratitude in my heart, I wrote, *"William, you came to serve, and you did serve us so well that we could not and cannot thank you enough to commensurate your unqualified service placed at our disposal."* May the souls of Kissiedu and William rest in perfect peace!

My family eventually moved to Okorase township so that I would be closer to the school. It would be a struggle every day, but I was determined to go. I did the best I could. The chief of Okorase, Nana Kwasi Brako II lived near the school building. Unknown to me, the chief had noticed me coming to school and leaving for home every day. He must have thought it was a painful experience for a young boy to endure.

The chief Nana Brako II summoned my mother to his palace and asked her to let me stop schooling. He added that my mother was piling undue stress on her young son, and instead of having to struggle to get to school every day, he thought it would be best if I stayed home. The chief meant well, yet somehow he saw all that I could become through the lens of the limited environment in which we lived. He even suggested that when I was a bit older, my mother could send me for shoemaking apprenticeship so that I could earn some money for myself.

My mother had not gone to school beyond some basic elementary level. Even though she knew she wasn't too far from being illiterate, she was stunned to hear what she thought was ill advice from a man who was highly regarded in the community, a literate and a former police officer. Of course my mother reasoned, he would know the value of education, so couldn't fathom why he would recommend I discontinue mine. My mother didn't see anything wrong with her son being a shoemaker; she just wasn't ready to define my future by the obstacle she didn't know when she would overcome. She wasn't ready for people who were not major stakeholders in her son's life to define his parameters for him. If her son was limited physically to go on expeditions to explore nature and his environment, she was of the firm belief that education could provide him the necessary wings or legs to do the expedition. This was going to go beyond my environment.

My mother urged me to try even harder, and at every turn reminded me that I was indeed, worthy. Worthy of excellence and worthy of achieving everything God had set in my heart. I was worthy because Christ's grace and sacrifice strengthens even the weakest person who latches his/her faith onto him.

He alone makes us worthy.

I never got the chance to visit Nana Kwasi Brako II to let him know what I had become, but my prayer has always been that my story will in turn ignite the hearts of young men and women who find themselves in desperate situations to push ahead, rather than settling where they are.

Everywhere I have been, there have been many people whose aspirations are shattered by well-meaning people. My prayer is that we would not let our dream suffer a stillbirth or a miscarriage by heeding the advice of people who do not carry the same passion we do. My mother knew this, that neither my disability nor my family's poverty made me unworthy.

For every day that I am blessed to be alive, I thank God that I get to share a simple message that you and I are worthy. We are worthy in the sight of God. Society can write you off, but that doesn't mean you should do the same to yourself. I am confident that Almighty God has put a great value on you and me, and even when our lives bring a huge setback, the blood of Jesus doesn't suddenly lose its power.

I remember vividly one Friday morning a few years ago while I was leading a prayer service at Covenant Congregation of the Presbyterian Church of Ghana, Dzorwulu-Accra. I spoke on the theme, "Do not worry." I referenced the scriptures, Luke 12:22-31.

> [22] *Then Jesus said to his disciples: "Therefore I tell you, do not worry about your life, what you will eat; or about your body, what you will wear.* [23] *For life is more than food, and the body more than clothes.* [24] *Consider the ravens: They do not sow or reap, they have no storeroom or barn; yet God feeds them. And how much more valuable you are than birds!* [25] *Who of you by worrying can add a single hour to your life[b]?* [26] *Since you cannot do this very little thing, why do you worry about the rest?*
>
> [27] *"Consider how the wild flowers grow. They do not labor or spin. Yet I tell you, not even Solomon in all his splendor was dressed like one of these.* [28] *If that is how God clothes the grass of the field, which is here today, and tomorrow is thrown into the fire, how much more will he clothe you—you of little faith!* [29] *And do not set your heart on what you will eat or drink; do not worry about it.* [30] *For the pagan world runs after all such things, and your Father knows that you need them.* [31] *But seek his kingdom, and these things will be given to you as well."*

It is refreshing to read how Jesus emphasizes that none of us are worth anything less important than the birds of the fields, and that should be a reassuring reminder that the God who takes such great care of the animals in the air is even more concerned about each and every one of us. God takes time out of His precious moments to ensure that the birds are fed, even though they do not have to lift a finger to sow anything or plant any seed.

Their worth cannot be compared to that of humankind—you and I. We have been created in the image and likeness of God. For every disability that makes us count another person as unworthy, or one that makes a person give up on himself or herself, I am glad that there is a loving God, our Father, who will always count us worthy, irrespective of the thoughts we and others have allowed to rule our lives. Perhaps, like in an analogy you have heard before, God does not focus on the container; He focuses on the content. His focus is on you and me. His focus is on the man and woman and boy and girl whom we look past every day.

It is heartwarming and encouraging to ponder the Bible story of Mephibosheth, the son of Jonathan who fell down as a little boy and was paralyzed for the rest of his life. A man whose destiny was supposed to be in the royal courts ended up in the dark and destitute corners of the city. Many years later, he found himself standing before King David, and could not possibly imagine anything good was to come out of that encounter. Mephibosheth had spent so much of his life in squalor that he had accepted his new identity. He considered himself to be "a dead dog." Even when the king revealed the reason for his invitation, and that Mephibosheth's life was to change forever, he was convinced that he did not deserve all the kindness bestowed on him by a king. The king thought he was worthy of every chance to fulfil his destiny, but Mephibosheth was convinced he was nothing more than a useless dog—worthless! A worthy individual, and yet he considered himself "a dead dog." My prayer is that all of us will see ourselves from God's perspective, and not that of society.

Through the years when it looked bleak in the life of my family, who wondered how they could make it through another day, they held on to the fact that I was not a residual value to be written off as scrap. The beautiful truth is that it is only God who does the evaluation of your life, not humankind. It is the Lord who gives strength to the weary and increases the power of the weak. He makes those who hope in Him take on wings like eagles, and soar over their problems.

I am worthy because God has given me a unique fingerprint and designed me to fulfill a specific purpose. For everyone who may have an ailment or terminal disease or physical or emotional handicap, the only reassurance is that God gives each of us grace to run our own race. If by God's grace, I could get on my feet again with the help of a walking stick, to help me go about my duties, then I know that God can give you the needed support in life to face the challenge squarely. God in His wisdom will harness the potentials, talents, gifts, and skills in you to make you useful to your generation and beyond. You are worthy.

Everyone is worthy in His image. Our potential in life is not limited because of whatever disability we have. It is the times that it seems like life has hit us out of nowhere and when it looks like the world is passing us by that we need to remind ourselves that you and I are indeed worthy. It is the times when the world has condemned us as an afterthought, or when the heaviness of an imperfect life makes us feel as though we are scrambling to find a reason to hold on, that we need to remind ourselves that we are worthy.

Nothing in the world serves as a reminder for this truth. Some of the richest people in the world give up on their lives because somehow they come to the stark realization that their riches aren't all there is to a fulfilling life. Many poor people give up on themselves because of the weight of their poverty. All classes of people in society go through every day with a myriad of challenges.

The comforting thought is that with our focus on the cross, we will be able to rest in the arms of God on the heavenly throne who knew who we would become even before He created the earth.

Feeling worthy is not an automatic feeling. In fact it is more than a feeling. It is in knowing in our hearts that we are worthy. No one automatically wakes up every morning feeling great. It takes conscious effort, even when our circumstances dictate otherwise. Our outward appearances may come with their own limitations, and hurdles. Yes, they are hurdles, but we can live past them, if we can find courage to embrace the fact that all our steps and moments are in the hands of a loving Father who cares about every breath we breathe.

This is why we can afford to encourage each other to step into God's grace and let our heartbeat remind us every morning that we are worthy. We have to tell our minds and our hearts, again and again, that we are worth more than the birds in the air; we are worth more than the lilies in the field; we are indeed worthy!

CHAPTER

12

INSIDE OUT

The Beauty of Tomorrow's Uncertainty

"Never since the world began has it been heard that anyone opened the eyes of a man born blind. If this man were not from God, he could do nothing." John 9:32.

Not long ago, I had the pleasure of listening to a Bible teacher ask a fascinating question of his congregation. The audience, who were cheering and clapping just moments before, were suddenly quiet. The question pierced them deeply. Each of them seemed to have come to a point where they had to respond as honestly as they all could, and it was rather remarkable. I saw the faces in the room, and each of them seemed to be wondering what the others were thinking.

The preacher asked, "Could it be that what we see as disability isn't what God sees as disability?" A simple question indeed. Yet it had to be one that we often never take the time to reflect upon. The thought behind the question must have been, "Could it be that our interpretation of a physical disability comes along with a label of insufficiency and maybe gradually nudges all of us to miss the mark completely?"

"Could it be that you and I have been so preoccupied with what our society has conditioned us to think that we cannot hear God's heart? Could it be that we ignore the beauty of God's perfection in our brothers and sisters and we, in turn, have been blinded in our hearts all along?" The simple question was intriguing and equally thought-provoking.

A disability has come to be interpreted by our communities to mean a condition which restricts a person's mental, sensory, or mobility functions to perform a task in the same way as another person. Reputable international organizations like the United Nations speak of, "any restriction resulting from an impairment of ability to perform an activity in the manner or within the range considered normal for a human being." The word "normal" becomes the window to a world where our own prejudices and stereotypes paint one another to fit nicely in our own worldview. But is it a definition that really fits the terminology?

What I found interesting through the years is how most people with different kinds of disabilities reject a definition pulled together by a team of doctors from the World Health Organization (WHO), and defined disability from a medical point of view. Sure, they mean well, but I have often smiled at the thought of Almighty God looking down at how we have the audacity to label one another. The medical professionals saw disability as a restriction, and a result of a medical condition. I can only imagine that an unintended consequence of this school of thought becomes society confidently seeing a man or woman who has an impairment of ability as less than normal. No wonder the rest of us can easily ride along with this definition and call a blind man or a deaf woman abnormal, strange, off, and unworthy.

Finding the courage to offer practical help to people who live with one type of disability or another is not a hurdle for one person, one group or even one community. It is one that every community must handle as best it can, accepting our brothers and sisters, sons and daughters as they would their own selves, and embracing opportunities to shake off any mental barriers we have erected to make people look different and strange.

A researcher once shared a simple yet profound thought, that perhaps because we are hardwired in society to believe that one person's gain is another person's loss, it is often a hurdle in itself to convince individuals that by doing our best to uplift one another, we will not be trampling upon our own happiness in the process.

A collective effort to see a beautiful tomorrow for every person we are fortunate to come into contact with will be a refreshing perspective, as opposed to our predisposition to cast away anyone whose physical or mental position doesn't fit our social construct. A government can indeed put policies in place, but it will take you and me, every individual to do his/her part to affect the change. Policies by themselves are beautiful and idealistic hopes. By themselves, they are words that, unless we latch on to them, and genuinely seek to embrace their meaning, won't make any difference at all.

I believe that when all of us together as a society work diligently to remove the barriers we have created as guardrails of our customs and comfort, our brothers and sisters who live at one point in time or another with some physical disability, will find a society where everyone is encouraged to do his/her best and become what God had created and destined for them to become.

Every day when I have had the opportunity to share God's word about his amazing grace, I challenge Christians to take the lead and demonstrate this grace and love to a world around us. While society continues with its quest for definitions to help shape our attitudes, there is one perspective that, irrespective of the differences between the academic definitions of disability—medical and social, brings both persons with disabilities and persons without disabilities together. There is one perspective that is not confined to research and statistical analysis. This is the Grace of God to all humankind.

More than anything else, I love that fact that God's grace to each and every one of us is not confined to a model. We do not need to attain a certain status before we can qualify for it. Nothing about our lives has to be perfect, for the God who created Heaven and Earth accepts us just as we are. Whether we feel broken on the outside, and shattered in pieces deep in our hearts, God does not filter us through his own list of models and prerequisites to call us His own.

Grace gives you and me the reason to extend a hand because we see the man and woman next to us just as we see our own selves. Almighty God breathed his life into them also and has a purpose for each and every one of our lives.

A story in the Bible illustrates this truth every time I pondered over it. If God could use four lepers who had been rejected by society, to save the same society that had shunned them, then that gives a stark reminder that His value of you and me is not restricted to our ability or inability to perform a certain task. If God could turn the footsteps of lepers into sounds of marching armies, sounds so powerful that another army would have to flee for their lives, His grace is sufficient to use every one of us to fulfill the purpose for which He created us.

God of grace, who is sovereign, can decide at every point in time the vessel that He wants to use. I have encouraged many people and groups that I have worked with that there is no need to nurture antagonistic tendencies and prejudice towards each other, because some lives may seem "battered." It is precisely that "battered life" that He indeed needs the most to share His glory.

When the Sovereign God chooses that "battered" life to be worthy of use, our criticisms cannot deprive that life of His grace. However strong or weak people perceive you and me to be, we must bear in mind that it is God's sustenance that carries us through. Not our own might. Perhaps it is for this reason that God does not care to use either the strongest person or the weakest person, but rather anyone who with a humble heart, who comes to Him and acknowledges that nothing about us can guarantee us the next moment of our lives. Only His grace does.

There are many examples of God choosing anyone He wants to fulfill His purpose. Most of them may not be the first choice of others. He will look at the heart and not our physical appearance. The fascinating truth is that none of us holds an advantage in God's eyes because of what we think we can or cannot do. Rather, it is our submission to God that will make the difference. This submission brings us to a realm of God's grace to encounter and experience His goodness. I pray that our mind's eyes will be able to see the goodness of God in His grace, and how He is faithful to help you and me do everything that lies in our strength to pull down the walls that divide us.

How much of every waking moment would we change if we could see what awaited us in the next turn? What would we do differently if we knew how much of our lives was to change, suddenly, overnight, or even in the distant future? How honestly can we fathom that our next moment does not belong to any of us, but rather it is undeserved grace that holds everyone in the palm of Almighty God's hand?

If we were to look back someday to see how much we have missed the chance to see our world from God's vantage point, would we look back to where we have come from and wonder what we could have done differently? Would we have given enough grace to other people we may have met who may have had their backs against a proverbial wall, and who needed us to help them take another step?

The great mystery of life is that our tomorrows are just like a story still unfolding. The truth is that if we knew what the next chapter will be, we would do everything that lies in our power to make sure that the fragile moments we hold on to so dearly today don't drive what we do tomorrow.

No one knows for certain what tomorrow holds in store for you and me, but we can live our best days today knowing that when the new day arrives, in whatever situation it finds us, we can stand with our heads held high because we have lived the best lives we could.

In our relationships with people whose lives are connected with ours, and even with those with whom we have no reason to cross paths, because we cannot know where tomorrow will take us, it is important that we learn to focus on the heart of a person, not his outward appearance and certainly not his station in life at one particular moment.

Regardless of who we are today or what our challenges can be today, there is nothing more reassuring than knowing that God doesn't make mistakes and certainly didn't create you and me as an afterthought. He will use every one of us just as we are, regardless of our challenges, for His own glory.

One salient note in Jesus' story with the man born blind was how after Jesus had healed him, it was the religious people who had the most trouble accepting it. In their own minds, they knew so much about the religion and dogma that they had spent much of their lives learning, that they forgot who they were supposed to be using that knowledge to affect.

In many instances which I have had the chance to witness, it has been most unfortunate to see how some people and institutions that claim to be the body of Christ find a way to stand on a shining pedestal, removed from the reality of the people who walk through their doors every day and every night. Many religious institutions have even earned the reputation as the ones that, even though they claim to pray the most, seem to be the same ones that criticize other people's journeys the most. Rather intriguingly, the only thing to criticize a person for is where his/her life stands in the present moment.

I thank God for His grace that sees beyond where we stand today and sees each of us for what we would become. If we can find a reason to lay down our religious robes and pick up the proverbial cross of Jesus, even for a moment, we can also truly affect the lives of the people who feel hurt, downtrodden and maybe even left behind in our communities.

We would reach their hearts because we would see past their present, into what God can transform them into tomorrow.

> *⁸ The neighbors and those who had seen him before as a beggar said, "Is not this the man who used to sit and beg"?*

Jesus healed the man by washing in the pool of Siloam. His neighbors who had seen him most of their lives had only seen him as a beggar. They knew him as a beggar. Now they were unsure of his identity, hence their question, "Is not this the man who used to sit and beg?" While some said it was the man they had always seen to be blind, the rest had a contrary view, advocating that he was only someone who looked like that man. In their minds, it couldn't be the same person. The man they had seen, whom they had also tagged a sinner because of his predicament, eventually spoke to solve the puzzle that his life and sight had been restored. It was difficult for his community to fathom a truth that only God has the power to restore beauty, even from ashes.

The beggar's plight was no different from that of the man at the pool of Bethazda who told Jesus that he had been by the pool for thirty-eight years but no one saw past his ailment to help him take the next step into a new day. He added that, when the water was stirred, he had no man to put him into the pool, so that he could receive his miracle and live again.

As I went through my own life, there would be several moments when I wished my mother were alive today to see what her son's life turned out to be. I wished she would see the worth of my life, one that she didn't abandon when times were much harder than what she had expected. In the same way, I wish I could see the faces of every child and mother and father with whom my life crossed paths many years ago, and share my simple story with all of them. I hope that in every corner in the world, the story about Jesus who went out doing good to show mercy to you and me, will remind people who find their physical or emotional condition pushing them to give up, that there is hope, a story only they can tell.

There is someone whose pain would find meaning with your pain and someone whose rejection would become a thing of the past if they heard your story. Not mine and not that of another person. All of our scars aren't for naught, and neither is the scar of the person we walk or drive past every day. Every wheelchair and the person whose life revolves around its wheels, tell a story unlike any other. Every walking stick and every white cane paints a picture of a journey unique to a person in whose shoes we may never have walked.

Even when our lives seem to have fallen apart due to some unfortunate accident or some illness, we all can use a reminder that God can still use it for His own glory. It is uplifting to know that there is no scar or blemish in our lives that is wasted if we can turn it over to God.

The remarkable story of Jesus healing a man who had been blind since his birth was not received kindly in the man's community. In fact, they did everything they could to discredit Jesus, and nothing the healed man said made any difference in their minds. Their minds were made up, and they were determined not to see anything worth celebrating.

The religious leaders went on to call Jesus a sinner and used their perception of him to persuade the once blind man to change his story also. His response was simple and incredible.

> [25] He answered, "Whether he is a sinner, I do not know; one thing I know, that though I was blind, now I see."

The men who interrogated him hadn't had to live with the weight of the blindness for all those years. They were looking at a testimony, yet too stuck in their own understanding to appreciate the miracle of the healed man. His scar was a powerful testimony to them and yet they were too preoccupied with their own wisdom to see it. When the men pressed for answers and emphatically stated why they thought Jesus was a fraud, I find it interesting that the man who was certainly not as learned as the religious leaders, was as fascinated with the details of Jesus' life.

> *[30] The man answered, "Why, this is a marvel! You do not know where he comes from, and yet he opened my eyes."*

In every community we come across in our respective countries, there are many whose disabilities have given them every reason to think that they do not quite measure up. Society helped to reinforce that notion. Religion didn't help to change that. Only grace changes everything. Only grace sees who we are becoming and knows that God who sees the heart of man, deals with us from the inside out.

All of us will get the opportunity to come across men and women with debilitating illnesses that had caused them to be bedridden or in wheelchairs. We may come across people who have suffered physical hurts due to war or accidents, who in one moment never could have imagined that their eyes or hands or legs may not function quite the way they once had.

In all of the people whom we meet, one thing is certain: there is more to the person than the outward appearance. There are many who have been told only to be ashamed of who they are, and the weight on the world is on their insides. The scars may be deep, but the most comforting news is that there is no scar that the grace of Almighty God cannot erase. Erase, not conceal.

Someday we will learn to make our doctrines truly reflect the saving and transformative passion of Jesus Christ and genuinely seek to change the lives of the men and women whose hands remain desperately outstretched for love and care. God is working on all of us, one day at a time, and from the inside out.

In God's loving hands I have come to find that our bruises, scrapes, and scars may just be the message. Instead of our own shortsightedness becoming the undercurrent of our tendency to shove people aside and conveniently sidestep the issue of disability in our communities, I pray that we choose to fight for people like Jesus would. I would encourage everyone to go out of their way to meet people in need because they are souls that Jesus paid for with His precious blood.

We don't get to choose the task we carry for God's kingdom. Instead of judging and ignoring people, we should be asking if this is an opportunity for a miracle.

The true test of our character will be how we treat the people we meet along the way. If we are to be disciples of Jesus, we cannot afford to live lives on our terms and tuck ourselves away from the forefront.

You and I will need to have convictions about what we believe and stand for, what Jesus stood for, and uplift anyone our lives can touch when we hear his/her heart's cry. There is beauty in all of our brokenness and our imperfections, even the ones that society constantly reminds make us unworthy. In the minds of a society of which we are part, we may not measure up because of our differences, but there is nothing more uplifting than the thought that Almighty God knows precisely how to bring out the best in His children, even when we least expect it.

He has called us worthy.

CHAPTER 13

SAVING HANDS

Scars of Old Age, a Miracle of Life.

¹⁶ Some of the Pharisees said, "This man is not from God, for he does not keep the sabbath." But others said, "How can a man who is a sinner do such signs?" There was a division among them. John 9:16.

"Let your old and sick father go back to his hometown to finish the rest of his life." Those were the words heard over and again by a woman who was caring for her aging father. Her heart sank every time that thought crossed her mind. That was all everyone seemed to be telling her.

Many communities across Africa have slowly become places where the lives of the old men and women have ceased to be anything but worthy of life itself.

For some unfortunate reason, many communities have managed to believe that a person's inability to walk as quickly as he/she once had or to function in much the same way as he/she had in their younger years relegates them to worthlessness. Gradually, our old men and women—our fathers and mothers—lose their worth in the eyes of their sons and daughters. Along with that, we miss the wisdom of their years, and the protection they would otherwise offer to our feet every step along the rough road of life.

The woman who heard people give reasons to give up on her sick father managed to stand firm in the conviction that it was her turn to do all she could to take care of her aging parent. Just like her, I am confident that God's heart is never turned against people who live with some physical sensory or cognitive impairment. Old age doesn't mean a person ought to wither away for the rest of his/her life. Unfortunately, in so many cultures and homes around the world, it is the case. Where we do not do so overtly, our actions and priorities speak loudly for us.

An intriguing character in the Bible is Moses. He is well known for leading the children of God through some of the most remarkable moments in recorded history. God didn't think twice about using him mightily, even in his old age of eighty when Moses himself thought his best years were behind him. As a young man, full of energy, he looked for God's hand in his life, but after many years in the quiet of the fields tending sheep, it was difficult for him to immediately understand why God would choose a man like him.

God is all-powerful and as long as you and I have breath, we are still valuable to His kingdom. As long as our fathers and mothers have air in their lungs to live another moment, nothing about their life's purpose is tainted because of how fast they can or cannot walk like they used to.

I love the story of Moses, old in age, having to stand before the pharaoh of Egypt, yet what reigned highest in his mind was the fact that he had a speech impediment. Almighty God was leading him to perform a mighty miracle that would live through the ages, and he wondered if he was worthy enough to do what God was calling him to. God did not disqualify Moses. Even when his own disability made him feel incapable, God assured Moses that he would be with him every turn along the way. His old age wasn't a hindrance but he tried using his speech disability as an excuse.

God used Moses to remind you and me that until we leave this earth, God still has an assignment for us to finish. A heavenly Father who is deeply concerned about every one of us, and who impressively knows even the number of hairs on each of our heads, is counting on you and me to be reminded that we are worthy.

Our elderly fathers and mothers do not stop being valuable cornerstones of our lives simply because they became frail with age. The wisdom in their experiences does not lose its ability to guide us into taking steps of our own.

Ghana is not alone in how we treat our elderly, especially when we have become the ones they rely upon. Yet, in a rather intriguing contrast, we often view them as the repository of wisdom when our backs lean against a figurative wall. When we are unsure of where to turn in our own lives, suddenly their experience becomes useful, until we find our way again.

I have seen how in some traditional court settings, the people involved are allowed to consult the *aberewa* (the old lady), for wise counseling. A person seeks counsel from the *aberewa*, to benefit from the depth and richness in counsel from the elderly and its indispensability in the society. In those communities, the elderly play special roles to hold the society together, making sure cordial relationships exist among individuals and families. But we quickly forget their worth in our daily lives.

As Ghanaians and Africans, though we cannot continue to neglect our responsibilities of catering for the elderly by using poverty and economic hardship as excuses, these are the real difficulties that stare into our faces and need to be addressed on our continent.

Providing pastoral care to the elderly members of our church in their homes is one of the humblest moments I encounter in my ministry, as it gives me the opportunity to ponder over life. Some of them live solitary lives and do not have caregivers. At times we have to look for a family member or a church member who lives close by, to find out what kind of help he or she can offer the elderly folk.

In some cases, those that are found to live in abject poverty are put on the church's payroll to receive a meagre allowance at the end of the month. This may not be enough to cater for the needs of the aged. The elderly also battle with loneliness, and interestingly, even the churches and community they belong to see them as an afterthought—that their work is done and their lives are over.

Over the years, I found that most of the elderly have the younger generations at heart and in mind, and would want their progenies to succeed. The biblical story of a woman named Ruth saw this and vowed never to part ways with Naomi, her mother-in-law. Despite all persuasions— understandably so—from Naomi, to go back to her family, Ruth saw an opportunity to learn from Naomi's journey. Naomi had lost her husband and two sons when the family migrated from Bethlehem to Moab, when Bethlehem was hit with severe famine. When she decided to go back to her native land, her daughter-in-law Ruth pledged to go with her.

Ruth was ready to sacrifice her nationality and religion in order to accompany Naomi, and give her the needed care. Ruth was going to a land where strangers were referred to as "gentiles" and where natives were cautioned not to marry strangers. But those were not a bother to her; her focus was on Naomi and Naomi alone. The older lady had arrested her attention, and nobody and nothing could stop her from attaching herself to her.

Their story continues, that when they came back to Bethlehem, Ruth continued assisting Naomi. She spent a lot of time working as a farm labourer, in order to feed herself and Naomi. This is one remarkable trail of devotion, understanding the value of caring for a woman who had spent all her life caring for her own husband, sons and daughters-in-law.

Not long had Ruth started working in Boaz's farm before he became interested in her and had her married, an opportunity she never dreamt of. I am fully convinced that it was her commitment to Naomi that opened this door of hope to her.

Through her faithfulness, Ruth and Boaz gave birth to Obed, and Obed was to become the grandfather to one of the most prominent individuals of history, King David. Ultimately Jesus would hail from such a lineage of faithfulness, sacrifice, and service. Ruth's commitment to Naomi was exceptional and unconditional. My desire is that we will emulate such attitudes.

One Wednesday morning in 2017, a few members of the local church took to the streets in the local community to administer the Lord's Supper or Communion to the aged congregants in their homes. We got to Mr. Abedi's house. Mr. Abedi was eighty-seven years old at the time, and that day, while we were administering the Communion, one of his grand-children, Amoateng visited. He was so touched to see us coming to give Communion to his grandpa, an event he had not witnessed before.

It was not long before the young Amoateng started shedding tears. No one seemed to be able to comfort him. After he had sobbed for a while, he collected himself and explained the reason for the tears. He said that it was the first time in his life that he'd seen such a thing: the leadership of a church was going round to provide spiritual oversight and was taking Communion to the home of the aged, in this case his eighty-seven-year-old grandfather.

His tears expressed mixed feeling, for he was also full of praise to see us meeting a spiritual need in the life of the old man. He saw that his grandfather had not been forgotten by the church that he had served with all his strength when he had that capacity.

In my own way, I believe it was also an opportunity to reflect on life at this stage. The lives of the aged are still considered as worthy as ever by their maker.

If we have every opportunity to care for them and remind them to finish strong, we should do all we can, instead of walking away!

> *⁶ Now the people of Judah approached Joshua at Gilgal, and Caleb son of Jephunneh the Kenizzite said to him, "You know what the LORD said to Moses the man of God at Kadesh Barnea about you and me. ⁷ I was forty years old when Moses the servant of the LORD sent me from Kadesh Barnea to explore the land… ¹⁰ "Now then, just as the LORD promised, he has kept me alive for forty-five years since the time he said this to Moses, while Israel moved about in the wilderness. So here I am today, eighty-five years old! ¹¹ I am still as strong today as the day Moses sent me out; I'm just as vigorous to go out to battle now as I was then. ¹² Now give me this hill country that the LORD promised me that day.*
>
> Joshua 14:6-12.

One of the Bible characters who inspired my faith was a young man named Caleb. He was among the twelve spies who were sent by Moses to survey the Promised Land the Israelites were going to inherit. When the men came back, the majority brought a gloomy report, indicating that there was no way the Israelites would be able to conquer the inhabitants of the Canaan land. They lost sight of who their God was and told everyone about the forbidding strength of the people who possessed the land.

But Caleb did not heed to that report and silenced them, saying, *"We should go up and take possession of the land, for we can certainly do it."* Numbers 13:30.

Because of his bravery and faith, God also honoured Caleb and promised him and his descendants an inheritance in the Promised Land. It was at this point that when he was eighty-five years old, and had still not received the lot promised him, Caleb went to Joshua to claim his inheritance. Joshua, who had been an aide to Moses, and was also one of the twelve spies, knew of that promise and therefore could not deny him.

Caleb requested that Joshua give him the hill country the Lord had promised him that day, and though Joshua knew and heard then that the Anakites were there and had fortified cities, with the Lord on his side, he, Caleb, would be able to drive them out as the Lord promised. These Anakites were giants and war-like, and their mere presence on the land of Canaan terrified the Israelites to the extent they regretted having made the exodus to their Promised Land.

In the majority report to Moses, the spies said that "But the people who lived there are powerful, and the cities are fortified and very large. We even saw descendants of Anak there." They concluded that *"We saw the Nephilim there (the descendants of Anak come from the Nephilim). We seemed like grasshoppers in our own eyes, and we looked the same to them."*

Joshua 13: 28, 32.

Though forty-five years had elapsed since that promise, Caleb gave an indication to Joshua that he was as strong as the day Moses sent them out to go and survey the land, and what the whole of Israel could not do forty years back, he was prepared to do. He would confront the giants and overcome them at the age of eighty-five. Joshua obliged and gave him Hebron, a city occupied by the Anakites. When Caleb conquered Hebron, we learn that the land of Canaan rested from war. Caleb, therefore, displayed an extraordinary prowess to ease the tension bedeviling the people of Israel about the Promised Land, and he silenced the Anakites. He brought relief to his people; he finished strong. He fought the dreaded giants and conquered them.

God worked a miracle through the old man. If God has not finished with you, do not write yourself off, for He gives strength to the wearied. A clear case was Joshua. Joshua might have thought he had advanced in years and therefore could not directly engage the Canaanites, to fully possess the Promised Land. God had taken them to the Promised Land, but large portions were still under the Canaanites. It was only a small portion that had been allotted to two and a half tribes of Israel. The rest, nine and a half, were yet to receive their lots. God then called Joshua from retirement, telling him, " . . . You are now very old, and there are still very large areas of land to be taken over."

Joshua 13:1.

Joshua had not finished his assignment, and God had to call him to duty. This campaign embarked on by Joshua was a herculean one, to bring the entire Canaanite land under the control of the Israelites. God called the old man Joshua to lead the onslaught. Given the opportunity, the aged can still contribute their quota to the welfare of their society and must be consulted to tap into their wisdom, experience, and strategy, if we are to build a healthy.

If God considers the aged as useful, then as a society, we must protect these God-given assets and give them all the support they need to live dignified lives as best as we can, and not send our mothers and fathers back to villages to wither and live the rest of their days in isolation.

There is a story made popular through the years, and many call it "The Starfish Story." It is about an old man walking on a beach one morning. A storm had rushed through the area and littered the whole beach with starfish.

The old man picked one starfish at a time and threw it back into the sea. A little boy who was also walking along the beach saw the man in the distance and wondered curiously what he was doing. There were endless amounts of starfish along the beach and it was not hard to imagine how long it would take for the old man to throw all of them back into the sea. But he did, one starfish after another.

The boy decided to ask, "May I ask what you are doing?" The man gently stood up and looked at the young boy in the face. With a little smile he replied that he was throwing the starfish into the sea from where they had come. He explained how the tide had carried them to the shore and out of their natural habitat.

Out of the sea and onto the land, the starfish was helpless, and it was only a matter of time before their lives would be cut short. They couldn't find their way to the sea. The man tried to explain to the young boy how the sun's heat would soon kill all the starfish along the beach unless by some miracle, they found themselves in the sea.

The little boy wondered, "There are so many of them, and maybe what you're doing would not even make too much of a difference." Then he bent down and picked another and into the sea.

He smiled back at the little boy, "It made a difference, at least for this starfish." Maybe the reason why society seems to shun the reality of the age crisis is that the task seems overwhelming and from where we stand, it appears there is no end in sight.

It is not impossible for God to use any one of us, even that old lady/man who seems helpless today. Rather than encouraging people through practical actions, at best, we have lengthy research, and other work by so-called experts, hence the execution on the ground breaks down even before it starts.

There is such a thing as overthinking a challenge, and before long we are constrained in our own thoughts and willingness to act. The truth is, you and I do not stand alone in a genuine effort to make a difference in the world to men and women who have to overcome one challenge or another every single day. Note that there is a close affinity between old age and disability.

If we can see ourselves as nothing but recipients of God's unending grace, we will truly be humbled by that very thought and allow that to direct our attitude toward the next person with whom we come in contact. For this, our obedience will be out of a delight to honor God's grace to each of us, not a duty.

God can use each of us, in spite of how old we are or how frail we have come, to believe in our own selves. As long as we have life, there are unique places and hearts in our own areas of influence and among the people to whom we are connected, for God to use mother and father to rebuild bridges that our pride and attitude have broken down.

I am indeed thankful every day that we serve a God who rewrites our story. He makes it possible to steer through a society where we are too often concerned with our own needs, and where we seldom take the time to put ourselves in the shoes of our neighbor.

CHAPTER 14

WHEN WE FIND OUR WAY BACK

Towards a Paradigm Shift

³⁹ Jesus said, "For judgement I came into this world, that those who do not see may see, and that those who see may become blind." John 9:39

Wouldn't it be a beautiful moment if we turned around and saw the person next to us just as Almighty God created him or her, rather than as how we've defined them for generations?

All of us have heard how we are products of the world in which we grew up and the culture that shaped our own mindsets. The men and women who lived in the same region where Jesus restored eyes and hearts were not bad people. They had spent all their lives believing one thing, and even the Son of God couldn't compel them to rethink some of their attitudes.

As it is in all of our cases, it is incredibly difficult to change our minds once they are set, and the powerful truth is that we are often unaware of the strands of thoughts that came together to give us our sense of reality and even our perspective in life. Altering behaviors is not the easiest thing for any of us to do, largely because after a while, some of what we would hope to change becomes the very thing that we have spent our lives perfecting. Despite this challenge, one thing is true: unless we take the time to ponder on how we arrived at forming our thoughts and perspectives, it is difficult to embrace any suggestion that forces us to rethink them. The good news is that where our own strength falls short, Christ's amazing grace steps in.

A child born into this world often seems to have a blank slate of a mind. It takes time for this young child to fully explore his/her environment. Even our idea of who we are will take years before we can come to terms with it. As children, our sense of being was colored with innocence, but it was like a sponge ready to absorb anything that came our way.

Our concept of reasoning started forming along the way, together with our sense of identity. Very soon our life script became a complex picture of the environment of which we are a part and the connections we made in our own minds. Not every one of those reasonings and connections went through a filter that forced us to ask why we believed what we did, or perceived people or actions the way we did. Gradually, one thought piled on to another, and a poor worldview was formed and entrenched to give us a sense of who we are.

The challenging truth of the reality is that not everything we have learned along the way is positive. I have come to find that not every attitude we have picked up along the way uplifts the person next to us, especially when part of our life script has given us ample opportunity to believe that they are less than, imperfect, or unworthy.

I heard of a fascinating psychological phenomenon many years ago when I was researching cultural affiliations and the perceived safety that we all get from feeling part of a collective, in thought or as a group. That was when I first delved into how all of us go through life in pursuit of ideas and opinions that validate what fits nicely in our worldview, and find every opportunity to push away anything that runs contrary to that view. Psychologists call this phenomenon "confirmation bias," and because of the remarkable power in each of us to fish for information to serve this purpose, it is just as difficult to willingly allow ourselves to uncover information that makes us rethink the way we have perceived our own attitudes, often for many years.

We get to make sense of the world when we look at it through the lens which we have gradually perfected through the years, except that it is only through God's grace that we can truly see clearly. Anything on our own is jaded and often self-serving.

Yet, once we have formed our reality, we can go through the rest of life on autopilot, and not question what happens around us. Sometimes, and conveniently so, we blame rather than try to change our culture. We explain to ourselves how everyone before us had done something a certain way, hence there is no room to alter our thinking. Unfortunately, some attitudes that were handed down to us leave out the ability to see other people as an extension of our own selves, and realize that their lives are just as meaningful as our own.

In many communities across Africa, and in fact all over the world, individuals who live with some kind of physical, mental or emotional disability are branded as imperfect persons. Our interpretation of what they have to endure every single day makes us think they have become nothing less than a burden for all others to bear. As erroneous as this kind of thinking is, this is what has been entrenched in our minds, and we act on it without even giving it a thought.

Researchers who have spent much of their time exploring the way our biases tend to confirm our existing opinions had one startling point, that once we have made up our minds, or our beliefs, it often takes much less effort to reinforce them than to rethink them. In a strange way, it is not surprising that we find whatever it is that we set out to uncover, oftentimes even it doesn't exist.

Confirmation bias finds a way to creep into all areas of our lives, often when we are unaware, and in many cases when it relates to our self-image. It leaves us with the response, "This is how it is supposed to be" in our minds, and so not many things compel us to dispel something that we have accepted as part of our worldview.

In places where some cultural attitudes push people with any kind of disability on to the margins of society, this confirmation bias nudges others to follow in the same vein, rather than pausing for a moment to imagine a world where we see every person as possessing the heart and worth with which Almighty God created them.

Unfortunately, shaking off any such phenomenon is difficult to effect in our own lives. There are many times when we find something we say or do contrary to what we probably meant to say, but unless we try our hardest to alter our deep-seated attitudes, those notions and sentiments will become the bedrock of our thoughts. The even more discouraging possibility is that our ability to do this will fall even shorter, but Christ's grace can guide our hearts to make the gradual change in mindset.

One thought that all of us are keenly aware of is that our view of life didn't just come out of thin air. We have spent many years amassing information and piling on one thought after another. Often, we search for the familiar to help explain the picture we have already painted, to help us make sense of what we already understand. This foundation makes the process of accepting a new reality difficult for all of us to absorb. The only unfortunate part of this reality is that our biases prevent us from seeing the world around us and the people whose lives are just as precious as our own, through an objective light.

The tragedy of allowing ourselves to see another person as unworthy often begins with our self-justification. It is a phenomenon that gives us everything we need to reaffirm our views in our own minds. We tend to justify, not only what we have come to understand as the truth in our societies, but also anything that creates a consistent thought pattern and order in our minds. Forcing ourselves to accept new information may be chaotic, even if for a moment. That is uncomfortable, and it is much easier to avoid that altogether.

No matter how important the new information could be, we find that our learned associations create a mental hurdle of their own, and are difficult to overcome. Parting ways with our established world view and the scripts that guide us to make sense of the world around us will take an incredible amount of self-awareness and a readiness to change. It takes grace.

Perhaps the first big step is, at one time or another, to see our own prejudices and confirmation biases which we are naturally wired to accept as normal, for what they really are. When it comes to people who are no different from you and me, we ought to make a conscious effort to scrape away the stereotypes that enable us to label them as unworthy.

Our culture and environment do such a phenomenal job of wiring each and every one of us, that to take the time and effort to force our brains to rethink what we have always found to be reasonable will come with internal discomfort, and if we are not careful, external disdain from those who our actions seem to tell to check their own.

Confirmation biases manifest themselves in all areas of our lives. That phenomenon is not a negative occurrence, per se; in fact, it is the same thing which gives us the cause to dig our heels into beliefs and social attitudes. This is where we run the risk of letting the wind that blows in the community around us steer our hearts away from seeing another person just as Jesus would.

Many researchers have mulled over why it often seems to be incredibly difficult to convince people to alter their mindsets. They are well aware of the fact that we all live with a strong drive to hold on to our-preexisting beliefs, because, in a strange way, it is those beliefs that serve as an anchor for our lives.

If we are honest with ourselves, we will admit that no matter how skewed our perceptions may be, often we hold on to them, or even dig our heels into them, to make us feel good about our own station in life. But that station could change in an instant. For every day that we miss the opportunity to acknowledge the biases in our own minds, the harder it is to pause for a moment to acknowledge that who we are and every breath that flows through our lungs are nothing we have done to deserve. It is only through God's grace that we go through moment after moment and see the dawn of a new day. That is enough reason to find the humility to see another person as God sees them, through lenses of grace.

I came to uncover how our own biases help us shape the information our mind receives, reinforcing those bits of information that we wish to be true. That is probably the reason why we can shut off our minds to the challenges that another faces, and rather than stand to uplift them, we allow prejudices to dismiss what we wouldn't want to change our worldview.

In the bible story of Jesus engaged in dialogue with some Pharisees, he affirmed;

> [39] *Jesus said, "For judgment I have come into this world, so that the blind will see and those who see will become blind."*
> [40] *Some Pharisees who were with him heard him say this and asked, "What? Are we blind too?"*
> [41] *Jesus said, "If you were blind, you would not be guilty of sin; but now that you claim you can see, your guilt remains."*
> John 9:39-41

What I found particularly encouraging in the story of the man who had been born blind, but whom Jesus healed to become a testimony to his community was the fact that God works in all of us, beyond what our own eyes can see. The gaining of physical sight by the man born blind was a very joyful thing to the blind and even humankind, but

Jesus' overall purpose was to provide spiritual sight to those who were in darkness, for he came that those "who do not see may see."

The man born blind lived in a hostile community that was not ready to share in his joy when he received his sight. He was subjected to all kinds of interrogations, and maybe that was because the people who had spent all their lives knowing him could not get themselves to see him any other way. It is intriguing to find how it was the man's lack of sight that enabled him to also discover who his healer was.

What the people in the community were conversant with was the physical blindness to which they assigned an erroneous cause. To them, there was a blemish from his physical deformity that had defined the rest of his life. Jesus corrected the prevailing ideology and added a truly remarkable perspective. The man born blind was healed by Jesus from both physical and spiritual blindness. In the end, it was those who thought they had sight (the Pharisees) that became sinners and remained in their sins, which were spiritual blindness.

Could it be that our own shortcomings may come from the fact that we are so confident in our own biases that we have chosen to turn our hearts silent to a calling from God to each and every one of us?

A few years ago, there was a story in a local newspaper in Ghana, *The Daily Graphic*, which showcased the gut-wrenching reality of men and women whose fate is resigned to incredible danger, simply because of how they were born. There are towns and villages all over the country where people who have some kind of physical disability are immediately banished, or even put to death.

The paper reported that there were seven communities in both the Kasena-Nankana West and East districts in the country's Upper East Region who came together to make a bold proclamation at a *durbar*. They declared an end to the "age-old traditional practice of killing children born with deformities." It took courage, it took an awareness of another person's pain and hurdles, and I believe that most importantly, it took grace. It took people with the heart that finds the worth of another person to embrace children who face challenges, rather than ostracize them.

Yet, these communities remain scarce across Ghana, and all over the African continent where children born with physical disabilities or deformities are labeled "spirit children" and become the focus of a demonic exorcism. It is sad to hear how in some places, people would become onlookers year after year as children were killed by people known as "concoction men" with the job of administering poisonous herbs to the babies.

This happened in villages where someone had convinced men and women that such babies did not deserve to live; otherwise they could bring calamities to their families. The communities who didn't kill the babies shunned them. The practice had been passed down through generations, and no one paused long enough to wonder what their own lives would have become if it had not been for God's grace that kept them. No one took a moment to imagine how none of us stands a chance for perfection in the face of almighty God, but even then, He loves us and cares about every single moment in our lives.

The truth is that what happens every day and year in the remotest parts of our world, happens just as easily around us, except that we are too blinded by our own social perceptions to even see. Many young men and women, children and babies are shunned in communities around the world, and we have found very polite ways of reminding them that somehow they are pitiful, unfit for any value, and undeserving. They quickly become outcasts in the only home they have known, and if they are bold enough not to flee their towns and villages, live with the constant stigma of being unworthy.

It was in 1962 when American physicist and philosopher Thomas Kuhn became a household name with his book, *The Structure of Scientific Revolutions*. In one remarkable work, Kuhn shared a lot about some of the underlying trails of the human mind, including what became known—even today—with the term "paradigm shift." In Kuhn's work as a scientist, he was sharing a thought on the changes that scientific element and scenarios go through over time.

These changes end up being either the kind that happen in discrete and specific moments in time, or revolutionary moments that tend to be the pinnacle of a time period. It was at the heart of this work that Thomas Kuhn shared his idea that "scientific revolutions that define history often are marked by paradigm shifts."

Paradigm captures a set of ideas or knowledge on how a thing ought to be done and gradually become the norm. Consequently, the shift has to replace that norm with another norm that uproots the current one and forces everyone to reimagine a mindset in a way they had never previously thought to do so. A paradigm shift, therefore gives us a new path to unlearn what we knew and substitute that with another. Relearning a brand-new attitude or accepting a whole new perception or belief becomes a difficult mountain to climb.

Changing our attitude and our viewpoint requires forcing ourselves to unseat the deeply held beliefs or expectations about what society thinks or how it acts. For the paradigm shift to occur, our world will have to unravel and be simultaneously put back together. We have to allow our own brains to go through the transformative process of accepting new information and allowing the information to make sense in our minds.

Often, that is where the challenge is. But the beautiful thing about our lives is that no matter what we cannot achieve on our own, when God's abundant grace kicks in, we get the ability to allow our minds to undergo this process. Our paradigms can indeed shift without us having to worry about losing our identity. This can be done when we decide to unlearn the negative attitudes that have characterized our society for long, and to adopt new and more humane attitudes that prioritize human dignity at the centre, irrespective of colour, gender, race, etc. One thing we cannot afford to do is to allow some of the unfortunate norms that have guided our society, simply because it was comfortable to leave them as they have always been, to rule our lives. There is the need for us to strive make the change, or the shift, and with the help of God's grace, we are well able and equipped to do just that.

We can shift our worldview and live a life that embraces the fragile hearts of our society and gives our brothers and sisters who are often marginalized in society a place to stand. We can shift our own worldview into one that uplifts the downtrodden, and challenge one another to strive to become everything God has created each one of us to become. We can shift our paradigm and change the notion that has convinced us that a person who is physically or emotionally unable to perform a task is unworthy.

It all begins with unseating the norms that have gripped all of our hearts and made us see the world through what our society has handed down to us. It begins with allowing Almighty God to give us a heart that sees every person as He sees him/her. It begins with an attitude adjustment that changes our tendency to see ourselves as better than someone else just because we can walk faster than they can, or hear better than they can, or see when they cannot.

Around the world, the unseating of our perceptions about individuals and their abilities happens one moment after another. Somebody had to remind globally celebrated musicians like Stevie Wonder and Ray Charles to sit behind the piano and share their view of the world through music. Their mothers and fathers did not find a reason to abandon them or consult a "concoction man" to exorcise them because their lives took a much different turn than what they perhaps had expected.

Changing the way we view our world and the people whose disabilities seem to have closed all doors to their future begins with the realization that all of us are still in the hands of Almighty God who has all power to awaken a gift from the ashes of despair. When we think all is lost and there is no end in sight, God reminds us that His grace, indeed, is sufficient to bring each of us to an expected end. The world celebrates a woman like Helen Adams Keller as an American author and political activist because even through her disabilities, she went on to discover her own talent and passion to shape minds around the world.

Helen Keller was born on June 27, 1880, in Tuscumbia, Alabama. Two years later, she fell ill and shortly after, would have to live the rest of her life blind and deaf. None of us can even fathom the remarkable turn of events. Her world was to change forever, but she went on to become one of the 20th century's leading humanitarians, lecturers, and activists. All this while she was deaf and blind.

By the time she died in June 1968, a few weeks before she was to turn 88 years old, she had lived a full journey of life and continued to make a difference in many arenas of learning. She lived every moment of her life in silence and darkness, but she lived.

Every boy and girl around the world has heard the name Ludwig van Beethoven, the renowned classical composer. Despite his hearing impairment, many of his great compositions came from the last 15 years of his life, when he was partially or even completely deaf. If we allow ourselves to see the miracle of every life through God's heart and eyes, we would find that there are many more Beethoven's we see every day, trapped in the lives of the dejected men and women on the side streets and the alleys of our communities, waiting for their turn to die. Rather than letting that happen, let us do our best, no matter how seemingly insignificant to help them to live again. They are indeed, worthy.

If there ever was a time of any grave importance for a society and church to reach out and connect with individuals through a lens of grace, it is now. The impact could have an incredible effect on every man and woman we find in our communities. I strongly encourage that we embrace the challenge to confront disability issues in communities around the world, as an urgent call to action. It cuts across the men and women whose plight is advertised, and those whose stories are ignored.

This issue of disability is more than a charge to protect our elderly populations in societies where we easily abandon elderly men and women as if they have nothing else left to offer. In circumstances where society gives reasons to see a person as a burden on society, it is my hope that this work would spur in all of us the courage to rethink our own perspectives.

We may have the best of intentions, yet even with all our willpower, there is little we can do that will make a lasting impact. But with the grace of Almighty God, we can begin the often difficult process of reshaping our own cultural values and outlooks.

The topic of disability is one that is conveniently shelved or shoved into a corner because we have determined as a society that we can afford to do so. From the boardroom to the religious leadership quarters and the high offices of political power, we have all grown equally numb to the plight of our brothers and sisters. Interestingly, we allow old traditions to dictate our view on disability in a way that we would never allow with any other aspect of our thoughts and actions. Unfortunately, our attitude breaks the heart of many whose value is no less than our own and who by one reason or another have a different challenge than you and I.

There are places across Africa and other parts of the world where civil wars and violence left people either emotionally or physically wounded, often with no relief in sight. After years of living with such discomfort, it becomes their new normal, in a world where every one of us is too busy to care about anything besides our own troubles.

I have heard many people say that our mind is the battleground where all of our thoughts and actions take root. Indeed, it is amazing to consider the tremendous amount of activity that occurs every second in our brains. It is no wonder that our brains are also the place of turmoil about what we would believe and the way we choose to see the world.

But it goes without saying that whatever we accept as the norm that is what will dictate our thought, our lives and consequently our actions. If there is anything worth a lasting thought for each one of us, it may perhaps be that allowing ourselves to rethink some of the strange perceptions we have carried throughout our lives will require an intentional change of focus. It is my prayer that our focus will be on the amazing love that we find freely in Jesus Christ, and the grace he is counting on you and me to extend to everyone around us.

Willpower alone cannot rewire our brains to see the world through the lens of grace. Our minds have every capacity to absorb the truth, but we have to be willing to embrace that truth and do the work of reshaping our perspective, through one encounter after another. Rewiring the brain's circuits comes with its own discomfort or even roadblocks. It is worth noting that for beliefs and attitudes planted firmly in our hearts for decades, it will take a little more than emotion to reset our own thinking.

It will take grace.

CHAPTER 15

WHERE GRACE LIVES

We All Fall Short. Never Too Late to Arise, Together

> *"As long as it is day, we must do the works of him who sent me. Night is coming, when no one can work. ⁵ While I am in the world, I am the light of the world."* John 9:4,5.

Even in our striving to do the very best we can, we miss the mark over and over. We will miss it because none of us in our own might is perfect. It is only through God's grace that our eyes are opened to see what the heart of Almighty God sees. Every one of us, from the young boy in school or at the playground, the teacher or doctor or lawyer, the market woman or the preachers, no matter our vocations, we encounter people whose ability to do something may not be the best. They could be old or frail. The person could have a hearing impairment or could be blind. Whatever their disability is, our minds and hearts have to be set on seeing them for the children of God they are, and rush to their rescue.

I am glad that the God we serve is one who understands our shortcomings, and that even when we haven't been the best we possibly could be to one another, he still hears our hearts cry. We may have turned a blind eye to the pain and frustrations of many people with whom we crossed paths every day, and not taken the time to acknowledge them. As long as there is today, a new day, we have the grace to live to share that abundant grace with one another.

Maybe we have walked past the man in the wheelchair and nudged him to the side so we can get to our destination more quickly. We may not have done anything overly malicious, but we have missed our chance to make a day a little brighter for someone who may need it more than we do. Maybe we have mocked the man whose ears cannot hear the sounds that fill our day. If that man had his own way, he would hear everything you and I hear, but for whatever God's purpose is, he has a different story. Maybe we have left our grandfathers and grandmothers in villages for them to wither and die.

Society may have given us the perfect excuse to abandon the people who need us the most in their old age. Maybe we have missed countless opportunities to show the heart of God to the people we have passed in many moments. Whatever the case, it is never too late to determine to impact a life. More than declarations and talk, let our life shine with our actions toward anyone whose heart's plea we could pause for a moment to hear.

All of us can make a commitment to see our world through the lens of grace, and it is my prayer that our failure to address the issues that plague our society will not hinder us from rising now. We can rise together, hand in hand. As we learn in life that we cannot make it in this life on our own, and not knowing who will be there for us someday, it is not too late to do our best to reshape our views.

Impairments, the frailty of old age, the suffering of men and women with debilitating sicknesses are not a judgment or a punishment from Almighty God. The blind man whose healing never came is no less worthy than the man who can see the beauty of the sunrise and the beauty of the sunset.

Not just doing miracles but being there for people and helping in everyday life, the Christian has a unique opportunity to lead the world. If our church's single objective remains for God to be glorified in everything we do, then we will always be reminded of the truth that there is no hurting heart or difficult position that the grace of God cannot reach, but God seeks willing hearts like yours and mine who will actually take a step.

Our prayer should be that God will give us His eyes and his vantage point so that we can see the world through them. If we see our fellow being through God's lenses, we will be able to reach the needy without passing judgment on them for whatever their challenge is. The people forgotten in society should not and cannot be forgotten by the Christian faith. If the world leaves everyone behind, we cannot, as a church, follow suit.

We are not slaves to social pressures, and the redemption through Christ's salvation should give us the courage to do the best we can to uplift the people who need it the most. They have scars that we can help erase, and our work does not only consist of performing miracles. If we can make one person feel worthy, in a world where so many pressures make them feel unworthy, God's grace will reach them at their point of need and they will be able to use their lives to reach their full potential.

Even when the clouds of doubt bear down on you and me, my prayer is that God will grant us the wisdom to uplift someone who has only known society's ridicule. Unfortunately, the culture in which I grew up in Ghana was no different from that of the Jews who lived in the time of Jesus, and who thought they had a perfect reason to discriminate against people they thought were less than them. Could it be that the hostile attitude that was meted out to the congenitally blind man may have been the same if it happened in our town, our city or community?

The goal of the church should be to illuminate God's glory, in God's way, not our jaded individual ways. Together, I am confident that we can lead the world through unfamiliar terrains like empowering our brothers and sisters and fathers and mothers who live with some physical or cognitive disability. Our relationship to one another and our desire to uplift should be based on the truth that the blood of Jesus still speaks, and God still restores.

Jesus taught all of us a remarkable lesson in his encounter with the man born blind, in that unlike his community who all this while had shunned him and branded him a sinner, Jesus stated that the man's visual impairment was not a result of some sin.

Jesus went further to reveal the real cause of the man's predicament, saying, "but that the works of God might be made manifest in him" (John 9:3b). This statement from Jesus came as a shock to the Johannine community because it was incomprehensible to equate disability with God. But at the same time, it also came to exonerate the man from being tagged as a sinner.

Unlike the man at the Pool of Bethzeda who, after he had been healed by Jesus, was cautioned to go and sin no more, this other blind man received no such caution from Jesus, indicating a zero correlation between his inability to see, and sin. Jesus, therefore, introduced something new as a reason for the man's disability. The man was not born blind because of sin in his life or that of his parents, but because God's work was going to be made manifest through him. In Jesus's shining example, we learn that it would, therefore, be prudent for any community to focus on God, rather than seeing sin in every disability.

It is amazing how many of us hide behind the curtains of theological discourse or unexamined tradition to push our brothers and sisters away from God's unending grace. These unexamined traditions about persons with disabilities abound in many cultures, thereby relegating the disabled to the background.

In her article, "The place of women with disabilities in Nigeria" Celine Ebere Osukwu wrote:

"In Nigeria, there are social stigmas associated with disability. Generally speaking, persons with disabilities are seen as "good for nothing" and viewed as objects of charity. The situation is worse in the cases of women with disabilities. Women with disabilities face double marginalization. They are discriminated and marginalized on the basis of their sex, that is being a woman and at the same time they are marginalized on the basis of their disabilities."

Nigeria is not alone in this reality. As painful as this occurrence is, it happens in more places and to more people than we would care to admit. Persons with disabilities are therefore tagged with all sorts of stigmas thereby curtailing their potential. The rest of society had concluded they had better things to do with their lives than pause for a moment to care for the need of someone whose situation make the routine tasks a bit more challenging than most.

This was no different from the Jews at the time Jesus was to bring a life-changing experience to the blind man whom they had convinced themselves to shove to the side. Even when he screamed to get Jesus' attention, the people around him chided him to quiet down. Sure, no one around him ever thought that someday, this opportune time would ever arrive for him.

This was their style, to prevent the man from expressing his religious thoughts about Jesus. This was unfortunate, and more so when they cast him out because, in their minds, he was not worthy enough to sit in the same arena with them. He was less than. His life was not worth the same grace that Almighty God gave so freely to every one of them. They were so convinced of the man's unworthiness that they urged him not to bother the one person who could change his life forever.

It is rather painful to find that the churches in different parts of the world have not been successful in genuinely addressing the sufferings of the marginalized, the poor, the blind, the deaf, and the physically and mentally limited people. Some of us continue to find clever way of quickly running back to lift the hearts that have been left behind. Others are yet even to recognize the need and the reassuring promise that together we can make a difference in the lives of the people we come across.

You may have heard of the story of a young boy who wanted badly to be part of a race. The only problem he had was that even though his heart was bent on participating in the race, he was physically challenged. He had spent years shrugging off the fact that he would never be able to run in a race like the other boys he grew up with.

The young boy summoned the courage one day to do the unthinkable. He registered for the race and showed up in a wheelchair to participate. He didn't want a pity party. He was not a charity case; neither was he trying to be an inspirational story. One of the other boys walked over to him. Fear overtook him in that instant as he saw the tall and strong boy walking in his direction as if to remind him of his disability. He was petrified and quickly began to tell himself that he had made a mistake. The boy walked up to him, and with a smile, he stretched out his hand. Then he said, "If you fall, we fall, we all fall together."

The other boys nodded, as another helped him get out of the wheelchair to the starting line. Soon the gun went off, and the boys took off running at full speed. Almost a second later, as if another gun had gone off as a reminder, they all froze, returned to the starting line and picked up the young man who was still at the starting line. The crowd cheered in an incredible display of togetherness and a sincere effort to uplift the young man.

If he fell, they all fell. If his heart was crushed, all of their hearts would be crushed. That was the decision the boys had to make that afternoon. At the moment, they couldn't bother themselves with the outcome of a race while one of the participants stood at the starting line.

Chapter 15: Where Grace Lives

There is beauty in a sincere effort to uplift the heart of people around us whose voices have been shred into pieces year after year. As a community, collectively, we often miss the chance to see every individual as a willing participant in whatever race we are engaged in, and to see their need as one that we will gladly address before we fulfill our own.

If there is one thing I have heard over the years more than anything else, it is that most people who live with one form of disability or another do not need pity or mercy. What would be incredibly uplifting for our communities would be a compassionate understanding and opportunities for every man and woman, regardless of their challenges, to develop their passions, vocations, and God-given abilities.

Over and again, society dismisses the plight of a man or woman who lives with a disability, because in our minds, they are not good enough, not like the rest of us. The characters in the bible story, except Jesus, by their actions, showed that indeed the congenitally blind man was a true outcast in the Jewish community. The disciples consigned him as a sinner, his neighbors betrayed him, the Pharisees attacked his healer and saw him as a lawbreaker and a sinner, the Jews doubted the man's healing and tagged him as a sinner, threw him out of the synagogue and even more remarkably, his own parents, for fear of the Jews, could not defend their son.

Yet, it was the man's disability that brought him closer to Jesus. Having experienced him, he was put in a better position to speak authoritatively on the transforming power of Jesus Christ. Persons with disabilities need not be sidelined in any discourse affecting them, their society and the church. Their identity should be respected in much the same way as those without disabilities. The church, therefore, needs to pursue an all-inclusive agenda to make sure that no one is left behind in gatherings of God's people.

It is a frustrating moment to have come to a place when we see how life has dealt us a hand that we could never have expected and which seems difficult to handle. It is in that moment that disillusion sets in;

we are discouraged and despondent as we live through the moments in a day that we could never have imagined would have been our portion. Someday, we will look in the rearview mirror of our own lives, and see that it was God's hands that carried us through every mile along the way.

The burden on God's heart for all of us is to live in His will, and make what is important to Him, our priority too. It is only through the power of grace that you and I can begin to see the person who sits next to us, regardless of his/her condition, in the perfection that Almighty God created them. It is never too late to stand up to be the hope God can use to transform a heart in our community, our country, or our world.

CHAPTER

16

SALT AND LIGHT

The Hands and Feet of Jesus;
Not what we say, it is what we do

³⁵ Jesus heard that they had cast him out, and having found him, he said, "Do you believe in the Son of Man"? John 9:35

A researcher once asked a poignant question that has stayed with me. If indeed twenty percent of our society deals with some form of disability, where are the twenty percent in our churches? Is it that many people have walked away from church, faith or God altogether? Or have many found ways to disguise their discomfort or hide in the backseats of the church auditoriums so that they do not attract any attention to themselves?

Disabilities in society take different forms. Physical disability tends to be the most obvious simply because it doesn't take much for us to see it with our own eyes. That reality is a bit different for people with visual impairment. But whether the person has some form of autism or bipolar disorder, there is probably nothing that cuts at the core of a person more than the feeling of being sidelined in the place they hoped would be welcoming.

There are many people who would rather sit in the quiet of their homes, than walk through church doors anywhere in the world, for fear of being the object of ridicule. That discomfort places a burden on people that most would rather avoid. Understandably so. The exclusion they feel from the church has almost nothing to do with what the church says; rather it is about what the church does.

It is in the actions that are shown towards the men and women and boys and girls who live with some physical, emotional, mental and any disability that forces them out of the places of worship.

The challenge for Christian society is to be able to strip ourselves off any iota of pretense and to step out every day to be the sincere hands and feet of Jesus Christ. Jesus looked for the marginalized and the excluded and did all he could to bring them comfort. Jesus didn't reach them from a distance; he touched them and genuinely sought to make a difference in their lives.

The Jesus whom we represent would listen, and stretch his hands and heart to anyone who felt the weight of a society that branded him or her a nuisance, or even worthless. In the Church, we often have learned responses to actions and circumstances. We have even perfected what to say and what not to say. Somehow the person on the other end has heard our voices saying the same words over and again, but has seen that our words do not lead us to act any differently. What we do as a church paints an incredible picture that cast a huge shadow over everything we say.

I heard a story of a church that set out to create teams that would go into communities to assist people who wanted to come to church but were unable to for one reason or another. A striking example is the leader of the church who would organize one-on-one prayer sessions for people who would otherwise be too frail or sick to sit through a normal service. Her approach was to take the time to create an avenue where a person or family would not have to worry about the challenges of the person they had to care for, decentralizing ministries to make worship relevant to the people who matter.

In their own way, the leaders, as is the case in some churches in communities around the country, do their best to be truly accessible. For many individuals, their journey feels extremely isolated, and if the church where they expected to find comfort, aggravates their own discomfort, it is not hard to imagine why many people would shy away from what the church has to offer.

Grace reaches out and draws near, and does not push away. Seeing our brothers and sisters through the lenses of grace prevents any thought that would cause anyone to be seen as less than you and me, and not worthy. It is my prayer that we will not be so wrapped in the promise of comfort that church and faith seem to promise in contemporary society that we ignore the great commission that God has called us to.

It is my prayer that avenues of worship will turn away from the prejudice that may be more in line with cultural attitudes than with what Jesus would expect of you and me. In our world where the superficial seems to reign and the appearance of anything supersedes the actual substance, there is always the temptation to see a person whose situation may be unlike our own as someone we should conveniently escape, while rushing to the company of people of whose journey we would rather be a part.

My prayer is that the Christian communities around the world, not only in Ghana and in Africa, will embrace the men and women whose lives are perhaps a bit more challenging due to some physical, emotional or mental barriers, as we would any other child of the Most High God. An embrace that says a person is indeed worthy, and not given out of pity and not out of charity.

After all, it is in the Church that we discover the matchless and priceless love of God that embraces every one of us, irrespective of our flaws and shortcomings. Maybe that is the lesson we ought to be walking into the world with, and apply it in our everyday travels. All of us are broken vessels that Christ restores unto himself, and our challenge is to welcome people into the household of faith with the same genuine love that has been extended to us.

Our work as Christians does not end at the doors of our church buildings. It continues. Our work is our lifestyle, beyond a role we play just for a moment until we revert to our original selves. God is counting on you and me to be willing ambassadors of His grace, to be the hands and feet of Jesus in a world that is desperate for precisely that.

In every disability, God who knows all and sees all, has every opportunity to turn a person's story into a testimony. Everything that happens to us is a platform upon which God's grace and love are showcased. We cannot afford to cloak ourselves in a righteousness that fails to recognize the fact that our brother and sister's journeys may require us to get out of our comfort zone occasionally to lend a hand. It is not for charity; rather it is the same loving hand that Christ extends to us over and again when we are unable on our own to reach where our hearts are set to reach.

I remember a few years ago, stepping down from a podium after a speech. The crowd gathered in the room instantly rose to a thunderous applause. It was humbling for me, but most importantly, my words about what the church had to do as the lighthouse to the world had resonated with the people who had come to listen. I remember at one moment standing next to Ebun James, who at the time was the Assistant General Secretary of the Christian Council of Sierra Leone. She smiled and said over and over how she was taking every word I had said with her back to Sierra Leone.

What I found out in the conference was how in Sierra Leone's case, a range of initiatives was coming from churches, social organizations and government agencies to create programs to rehabilitate victims of civil war. The West African nation had lived through a period of enormous pain and disaster when a civil war broke out in 1991, and pummeled the country until 2003. By then the casualties had become the society itself.

Some of the most heartbreaking headlines had been the serious atrocities that were inflicted on the ordinary citizens of the country by the rebel forces, most notably the Revolutionary United Front (RUF), headed by Captain Foday Sankoh.

My colleague Ebun James recalled how RUF forces amputated many of its victims either at the wrist or elbow level and left them to bleed to death. Adding to their brutality and horrific actions, they coined the terms "long sleeve" and "short sleeve" to mock the deformities they caused. Subsequently, Sierra Leone quickly became a country with a high number of its citizens suffering from various degrees of disability. The society was handicapped in every direction and there seemed to be no hope in sight.

As I spoke to James, she surprisingly talked about what she admitted had become her own limitation. Her life hurdle had become the low self-esteem that was prevalent in some victims who lived with the aftermath of such horrific events. The organizations in the country were all scrambling to find any semblance of a solution for the many people whose lives had changed forever because of the enormous weight of their physical disabilities that they carried with them.

What was true was while the organizations needed every funding and strategy to begin a healing process, the church didn't. The body of Christ had the benefit of God's amazing grace, through which even in their lack, they could reach out and be a light in the community that was now filled with darkness. The brightest lights can still shine amidst incredible sadness, and I am thankful for the lives of people like Ebun James who lived their lives as a reassurance of God's abundant grace that has every power to restore.

Even in countries like Sierra Leone, where you and I would imagine the society would understand the plight of many of the people who lived through the country's dark hour, a person's physical disability continued to be a barrier of exclusion. These countries and others had ratified international agreements such as the United Nations Conventions on the Rights of Persons with Disabilities (UNCRPD), yet despite this, the persons with disability continue to suffer segregation, discrimination, and a myriad of disadvantages.

But as a body of Christ, we have a great opportunity to show love more than anyone. There are many men and women across Sierra Leone and indeed all over the African continent who scream every day for a hand that would actually stretch out to inspire and uplift. The cry is for a heart that understands the magnitude of change we have to make, to truly become the hands and feet of Jesus.

Amidst all the uncertainty and the chaos, the churches in Ghana and across Africa still have the opportunity to extend their *diakonia* to persons with special needs, who in many other circles, will be left to watch life from the sidelines. There are hundreds and millions of people with various needs who have been marginalized. These include the persons with disability, drug addicts, persons living with HIV/AIDS, and persons with chronic medical illnesses. Many have needs that the government and the civic organizations are still seeking the appropriate avenues to address.

The Church happens to be the place where the indelible image of grace and care ought to be found. It is often the place where the weakest among us, the frail, and the dejected, seek comfort. The Bible reminds the body of Christ that God's embrace is always available for anyone among us who is "weary or heavy laden." In the presence of Almighty God, the man and woman and the boy and girl whose hearts are heavy with dejection and filled with the weight of the world, are supposed to "find rest."

Creating the infrastructure to care for people who deal with one form of disability or another is understandably a costly adventure for churches, but there are still many who walk through the church doors every day who only yearn for a warm embrace and a reminder that they too are not forgotten.

Unfortunately, even within churches, subjective perception of the persons with disability has led to serious injustice. I know of cases where some persons with disabilities who wished to become ministers of the Gospel were denied ordination by their various church authorities, with no explanation given. A past Programme Executive of Ecumenical Disability Advocates Network (EDAN) of the World Council of Churches once shared his own experience with us. When he intimated his intention to become a priest, his church immediately offered him a scholarship package to go and study abroad, hoping by the time he came back, he might have completely given up the whole idea of becoming a priest. He did not accept the offer, for that was not his heart's desire; his heart's desire was to accept God's calling on his life, but in this, the church obstructed him.

This is just one of the many cases happening to persons with disabilities who feel called to enter the ministry. The irony of it was the fact that he became a lecturer at a theological seminary in Limuru, Kenya, where ministers from many denominations were trained (which probably included some from his denomination) to serve their communities. Somehow the very individuals who learned from him found him unworthy.

The Church is placed in a remarkable position at this time in history to be able to become an example to its communities, to help change the story of a society that often ostracized its own. The church can afford to ensure that provision is made for persons with disabilities to have access to places of worship without any difficulty.

When individuals in the churches discuss the needs of their members, the church would be well served to include people who can share the viewpoints of those with physical or emotional limitations or the elderly men and women whose lives feel like all their value drained away years ago and left them with nothing left to offer.

I challenge all of us to find ways that each of us individually, and collectively as churches can ensure that our communities see the exemplary truths of God's word in our lives. The urgency for this hangs on the fact that persons with disability are perhaps more likely to be atheists or be persuaded to abandon God's love altogether.

One powerful truth is that a person's disability doesn't automatically make him/her incapacitated. This is probably one of the least advertised realities of life, because our mind probably shuts down any further dialogue the moment we learn that a person has some emotional or physical disability.

It is indeed true that a disability will limit a person's capacity to undertake some form of major life function, whether that limitation is in seeing, walking, hearing or something else, but that does not in any way make him/her worthless. Society has a way of affirming that in our minds, but we would be well served to understand the truths about disabilities.

In my own life, I have come to find how a single moment can change a person's life forever. The great news is that regardless of what alters our plans and paths, these are never detours from Almighty God's plan to bring every one of us to an expected end.

Disabilities are certainly not foreign to our human experience. Apostle Paul, a prominent personality in our Christian faith, mentioned "the thorn in the flesh" purported to be his own disability while he pressed on to accomplish the work for which God had called him. In a humbling way, Paul reminds you and me of how our own disabilities ought to serve as a constant reminder of the frailty and dignity of human life. All of us are vulnerable in any moment, and that alone should be our guiding hand to open our hearts to men and women who call out every day for God's outstretched hand to bring them some comfort.

It is one thing to preach grace. You and I will have to step out of our churches and homes if we truly want to translate our sermons into actions. It may be the case that many people in our communities, whether or not they have some disability, will not see Jesus unless we are able to translate the message of grace with our actions. That is when we get the opportunity to shine the light of hope into our world.

In every community and country across Africa, there are still many people who may live with some form of mental, visual, physical, hearing, or cognitive disability. They are cast aside or even cast away by a culture that hangs on to its beliefs, especially those that feel comfortable to the majority. That attitude trickled into the churches also, and in no time, there was no distinction between the attitudes of Christians who have seen the worth of grace, and the secular world whose decisions are often guided by norms and policies.

Places of worship often tend to lag behind in their response to the needs of people whose plight doesn't immediately jump to the forefront. Along that spectrum is a very intriguing notion that all churches have to do to address the disability issue is to erect ramps for wheelchairs and modify their architecture. The ministry, however, transcends architecture. There is a greater need for all of us to strip away the fences that erect themselves around us to push away people who have disabilities. Instead, what our mind should be set on, is truly appreciating the grace that we have been given, and extending care to everyone as a child of Almighty God deserving our respect and our love.

> *"When we think of persons with disabilities in relation to ministries, we tend automatically to think of doing something for them. We do not reflect that they can do something for us and with us . . . they have the same duty as all members of the community to do the Lord's work in the world, according to their God-given talents and capacities."*
> —Pastoral Statement of U.S. Catholic Bishops on Persons with Disabilities, 2001

Our call to be the hands and feet of Jesus should be one that empowers and uplifts, rather than one that sets out to shower pity on someone.

Each one of us has a responsibility to refrain from peddling the same stigma that has plagued our society, and use our words and actions to value every life we are fortunate to come across.

In the days of Jesus Christ, the religious leaders and their communities had their own challenge of showcasing the love of God and His grace to people outside their temple walls. Their community often called people with any kind of disability unclean, and unworthy. Their disability was a blemish and a curse to them, and they were not interested in asking the simple question, "How would you want to be treated if you were in their shoes?" It would take Jesus who embodied the steadfast grace to set a change in motion.

As we go through our own Christian walk, my encouragement is to be mindful of the impact our actions can carry in our societies, and dare to step out to become the hands and feet of Almighty God. What can the Church do?

I pray that God's truth will continue to stir our searching souls. I have come to believe that we cannot make it out of the locked door of our social attitudes by our own might, but we can make every change we surrender our hearts to if we genuinely commit our steps to our chain-breaking and life-renewing Father.

In a world where it is often easy to overlook the obvious, and instead spend our energy looking for something hard and unusual, and even extraordinary, my prayer is that God will grant us the heart to see the simple moments around us where we can make a difference in the lives of the people we encounter.

CHAPTER 17

Our Declaration

Surrender All, Withholding Nothing

²⁵ He answered, "Whether he is a sinner, I do not know; one thing I know, that though I was blind, now I see." John 9:25.

Society doesn't have any obligation or expectation to see each person as being worthy in the eyes of Almighty God. But the Church does. Society does not have any urgency to mend hearts or pull individuals who see derogatory words or actions heaped on them out from under that weight. But the church does. It is amazing how many people we could find who see the church and Christians as the last group of people they would imagine reaching out to them.

Maybe it is because we are so consumed by our own needs that we forgot that we are not in the community alone. Perhaps in the Church, all our attention is so fixed on our own healing, our own prosperity, our own miracles, that we can easily overlook the miracle in the person sitting next to you and me whose situation is much different from ours.

The drumbeat of criticism against the Church seems to be about how everything the Church community ignores, turns into sheer insensitivity and is un-Christ-like. Disability doesn't have a stereotype. It can happen to anyone at any moment. In one instant, regardless of a person's health or economic status, you and I could be sitting on different sides of the church pews. Every moment we have is only temporary, and if we treat it as such, we are more likely to appreciate the breadth and strength God has given to us to carry his message of hope and grace.

As Christians, we get a rather unique opportunity to witness the message that transforms hearts and minds. Our words and actions ought to interact with other people's experiences in a way that illuminates the unconditional love of Almighty God. We get the privilege of being the hands and feet of Jesus.

As young boys in church, we sang a popular song whose lyrics unapologetically emphasized the great lengths God goes to reassure you and me that He cares about us. He cares about the sparrow and the bird and the animals in the field, while we never stop to wonder what their lives are worth. God cares for them; he knows all of them. God cares about you and me, and we are not disqualified because of a disability.

On every road which I have been fortunate to travel, one thing that is evident is how missionaries have tried their best to fill in the gap in places where society seems to have turned a blind eye. But it is not only missionary organizations' job to mend every broken heart or reach the people who are neglected by society. As Christians, we all have a role to play in this endeavor, and God is counting on you and me today.

A school of thought would argue that there is nothing more disabling in the body of Christ than to embrace a skewed theology that paints an individual with disabilities as an object. Beyond the compassion to ensure that a person is not left out in the cold, I can only imagine how many people would love nothing more than not to see persons with disabilities in the Church as an unanswered prayer.

I remember vividly walking into a hospital room in Ghana to pray with a Christian family that was going through a medical crisis and on the verge of giving up. God must have had a sense of humor because he sent me. It might have been a humorous moment in Heaven because maybe the family's heart could not fathom that God would send a preacher with disability to pray with their family. Maybe in their minds, they needed someone they could be sure had no infirmity, not me. I understood their reasoning. They had read the same Bible I held in my hand. The encounter where Jesus met the blind, deaf, or lame and restored them seems to have stuck in their minds. They could not fathom a God who would not do the same for everyone. Unfortunately, that is a theology that has reigned in our churches and in our communities, that God must heal the sick by all means. But note that healing goes beyond the physical, and one should not limit himself or herself only to the physical healing. God uses me to minister to people not because of my physical disability, but in spite of it.

God wanted to remind this family that it is He who heals, and can use any vessel He chooses. This was not the first time I had prayed for the sick to get healed. The power to heal does not come from me; it rests with God. God therefore should be the focus and not me. Though I also look forward for my miracle, since I also believe in miracles, I have grown in my Christian life to understand that, the only time God actually promises complete healing is where "he will wipe away every tear from their eyes, and death shall be no more, neither shall there be mourning, nor crying nor pain anymore, for the former things have passed away." Rev. 21:4

Beyond any shadow of a doubt, Almighty God is the potter and we remain the clay. He alone chooses what to mold us into, and nothing He does is an accident. There are no mistakes in His nature, and that is why I can stand on the infallible word of God to share the news that

God has each and every one in His perfect will, and no matter what happens in our lives, we will never stray from His hands.

Once I was heading home from an international conference when I made a connection at Dubai International Airport, one of the world's busiest. I ran into my friend Kwadwo Amoah, who was returning to Ghana from China. Kwadwo had been a Christian student leader at the Kwame Nkrumah University of Science and Technology, at the same time that I was at the University of Cape Coast, playing the same role.

We had met a couple of times at National Union of Presbyterian Students-Ghana (NUPSG) Conferences so we had a lot to talk about, as it felt like many years since we last spoke to each other. We recollected those times when we were moving from one campus to another, organizing the young Christians, inspiring them to remain steadfast in the Lord. We were doing this through drama, choreography, music, and religious rallies. In all these, little did we know that God, in His own wisdom, was preparing us for His higher service.

Kwadwo had gone to China to pursue further studies to become more efficient as a church administrator at Presbyterian Church of Ghana, Grace Congregation, Akropong, where he had been employed. I was also returning from a World Council of Churches Conference in Colombo, where I had challenged the leadership of the various churches worldwide to emulate the example of Jesus, and to concern themselves with programmes that would empower the less privileged in society.

Kwadwo and I are still clay in the Potter's hands, and even as we swapped testimonies on what we have come to see and the invisible hand of God at work in both of our lives, we reaffirmed for each other that He is molding us into any vessel that would make us valuable to him. It was truly refreshing to retrace the steps God had taken us through so that we could share our stories again. I thank God that He counted us worthy to be used to affect the entire world for Him, and praise be to His name.

Can our society follow Jesus' example without being strapped by our own learned attitudes and cultural misconceptions? Can the church find the grace to genuinely seek to reach the hearts of the men and women who feel downtrodden and beaten down by diseases, failures, disappointments, rejection, and disability?

Our attitude can get in the way of God's agenda, especially when we are busy finding reasons why others are unlike us or live with one challenge or another. With his own example, Jesus opened a new chapter of understanding disability.

One of the remarkable eye-opening encounters for me, was finding how many men and women with disabilities are not sitting in line waiting for anyone's sympathy and recognition as charity cases. There are many who have not resigned themselves to their limitations and have given up on themselves because they are blind, or deaf, or have one form of disability or another. The challenge is to every one of us to walk a proverbial mile in the shoes of our brothers and sisters to see the world from their vantage point, and then do the best we can to reevaluate our own perspectives.

I am of the opinion that this ought to be emulated by all Christians, to get closer, identify with, and advocate for persons with disabilities. We can only do this through a prism that is not blurred by social stigma and cultural behaviors, but made clear through grace.

I encourage each and every one of you, as Christians, to take on the challenge of retelling the story of grace to a world that is waiting to uncover the truth that no matter a person's seemingly outward imperfections, there is no blemish in the person's heart that would make God want to discard him or her. God alone is capable of leading you and me, and everyone, regardless of our own shortcomings, to a destiny he has called us to. He is still in the restoration business and can mold every one of us back together, much better than you and I can even imagine.

I am confident of this also, that you and I can, in our own arena of influence, do our part to confront society's entrenched cultural attitudes, and retell the story that every one of God's creations is indeed full of passion and full of life.

If God can make dry bones rise again, he can use every one of us irrespective of our disabilities and our shortcomings. In the eyes of God, we are precisely how He wants us, and not a day goes by that He is surprised by our condition.

I thank God every day that I have been afforded the opportunity to tell a story I otherwise wouldn't have been able to tell candidly. I have gone through my own path in life to discover that if a person cannot see with his or her natural eyes, that doesn't mean God will leave him/her alone. The fact that a person cannot hear the sound that fills the skies every new day doesn't mean God will stop speaking to his or her heart. In fact, the magnificent God who is the master potter of all of our lives has His eyes on even the sparrow on the field. That, to me, serves as a powerful reminder that He didn't stop caring about you and me because of our disabilities.

God didn't stop caring about the young man and woman on the side of the road whose disabilities have left them feeling worthless and thinking their best years are over. For a God who specializes in taking our weaknesses and using them for His glory, He alone knows how to set treasures in jars of clay that He alone can mold to perfection.

I can only hope that this uplifting message will reach every disabled person everywhere in the world: that God didn't lose sight of his/her plight, but instead He reassures us that every one of us is counted worthy to Almighty God. I have never been more encouraged than I am now, that there is a God who will take what may seem as broken vessels and restore every piece of them.

CHAPTER

18

WORTH FIGHTING FOR

God can use Anything?
Can He Count on You and Me?

³⁶ He answered, "And who is he, sir, that I may believe in him?"
³⁷ Jesus said to him, "You have seen him, and it is he who speaks to you."
³⁸ He said, "Lord, I believe"; and he worshipped him. John 9:36-39.

A powerful truth that I have seen manifested over and again is the amazing testimony from the lives of people whom society would have at one time or another written off. There are the people who either through an issue at birth or an accident along the way have earned the label "disabled." Someone concluded that their lives did not measure up to some standard in society. Perhaps no one knows their story or how they got to sit on the corner of the street, but we have cast our vote on their future.

Sadly, we all happen to be products of a society that has little remorse in defining a person's limitations, rather than finding a way to erase them. We know nothing about how a man lost his sight, or how another lost his hearing. We may not have stopped long enough to wonder how an able-bodied man burned the flesh that once draped his body. We do not know their story, but somehow society determines they are not worth our time. All of us can think back to a moment when we may have counted someone out or when their presence meant absolutely nothing to us.

Some are young, others are old. Some are rich, but often, most are poor. Their voices are muted because they may not have enough wealth to attract a simple smile or even a kind word of encouragement. Their reality may have come with its own set of challenges and obstacles, but there are also many of these men and women who somehow manage to live another day and go on to tell stories only they can. Some live through unimaginable odds to find their voices and their hope.

I found in the incredible testimonies of the people who at one time or another felt marginalized and rejected, that there was also so much potential trapped in their hearts. They also carry a hope that someday a God whose grace is sufficient for them would find them, and find them worthy enough to turn their lives around. But maybe, God is counting on you and me to be His hands and His feet to our brothers and sisters.

These men and women, boys and girls whom society—consciously and otherwise—pushes aside to the margins of life, are the ones God will count on you and me to find and restore. Perhaps there is nothing that would make a bigger difference than courage, to alter our own mindsets, against what our own humanness and environment have defined for us.

The story of the blind man in the Bible called Bartimaeus is as powerful as it is relevant in our society today. The message rings loud, but the only question is, who would listen? Bartimaeus had heard that Jesus would be passing by where he sat and imagined this would be the perfect opportunity to get his miracle. He had been blind for many years, but that moment was a time that he had determined he would change his lot in life.

Without knowing which direction to turn, Bartimaeus reckoned if he couldn't see Jesus, he could shout loud enough for Jesus to see him. The great lesson is from a man who despite his disability was aware that all his abilities in life were not muted. Rather than being constrained by his obvious challenge, he resolved to do what he could do. He may not have been able to see, but he could talk. In fact, he knew very well that he could scream, so he did.

While Bartimaeus was doing all that he could to attract the attention of Jesus, his own neighbors whom you and I would imagine would have urged him to get his miracle, obstructed him. Perhaps in their minds, there were more important people for Jesus to see. It is interesting to think that perhaps they reasoned there were more pressing issues for Jesus to address.

In their eyes, Jesus had better things to do with his time than to waste it on Bartimaeus. Yet he was determined to never give up, he fought and fought till Jesus stopped for him. Jesus knew Bartimaeus was worth fighting for. It is rather intriguing to fathom the idea that Bartimaeus himself also must have believed that he was worth fighting for. As his name intimated in Greek, he was the son (bar) of honor (timaeus). Bartimaeus therefore was worthy and was worth fighting for.

Anytime I have recalled this story, I am encouraged by the fact that Jesus did not walk past the blind man because everyone else in his community thought he was a nuisance. In much the same way, the body of Christ, the Church, can set a powerful example for the rest of society to follow. Starting with the confines of the Church and its doctrines, the love and grace of God have to find a seat. True grace has to permeate our hearts beyond our own selfishness and politics to reach the people in the community who scream both loudly and quietly for Jesus and his Church to hear them. My prayer is that grace find a seat in you that is high enough to make the needs of individuals your priority.

Often with our words, our actions and our attitudes, many of us lose sight of the fact that it is indeed only God's unfailing grace that makes every individual, no matter his/her physical or mental condition, worthy. God's abundant grace that shines onto the wisdom in the hearts of our elderly men and women, and the faith of every boy and girl whose physical impairment has once been their limitation, inspires them to find value in themselves again.

One's worth is not limited to what he/she can or cannot see, what he/she can or cannot hear, or how quickly he/she can or cannot walk up a hill. Every life, no matter its condition or fragility, indeed, is worth fighting for.

Occasionally, I think about a young woman whom I knew years ago, Esi. She had once been an enterprising Ghanaian lady, full of life. She traveled to London where she fell in love with a young British man who also fell head over heels for her. Her bliss was unfortunately short-lived and what had once been a beautiful life was seemingly coming to a grinding halt.

Putting the pieces of her life back together turned out to be an incredibly difficult task, and soon, she had given up on herself. Esi tried her best to numb the pain and drape a curtain over her troubled marriage as best as she knew how. There had been people in her life, and people in churches where she would attend every Sunday, but no one saw that her heart was bleeding to death.

Out of the blue, I received a phone call one evening. Esi had become destitute and decided she wanted to end her life. She did not think her life was worth anything, at least not to her. The only hope I had to share with the young woman was from my own journey and the nuggets of inspiration I had come across along its way. There was an Almighty God who was truly loving, and truly interested in putting broken pieces together. All I could do was share what I know; it was God's work to convince her heart to hear.

My hope was that Esi would be assured of her worthiness to God. The same God, whose eyes know every hair on our heads, and who keeps close eyes on every bird in the open field, surely, knows Esi, and cares about her life. My encouragement was that no matter how battered one's life had become, and how worthless we become in our own eyes or even those of the society around us, there is nothing that is beyond the reach of the precious Lord Jesus.

God restores. Jesus' life is filled with story after story that even when everything in our life points to hopelessness, there is a grace that brings us back unto Him. There is no example perhaps more striking than Jesus hanging on the cross at Calvary with nails piercing through his hands and feet, and blood gushing from his sides; yet He turned to the man who was to die on the cross next to him, and extended grace. There is no circumstance too extreme that grace cannot begin the work of pulling our hearts together, to live our best lives that will bring God all the glory.

I spent the rest of the night awake, praying for Esi that somehow she would accept the outstretched hand of God's grace that redeems and resets even the moments when we think our situation is too far gone to be worth anything. The night before, she had convinced herself that suicide was the best option for her. She chose to live, instead. She did not have to drink the poison or follow through with her other idea of drowning in the nearby River Densu, near Weija, Accra.

All of us come to different crossroads in life when we often have to dig much deeper to remind ourselves that we are worthy just as God has created us. Our failures do not erase our worth. Our disabilities do not wipe away our value. Maybe we can become reminders to one another of this amazing fact. Maybe you and I can take on the challenge of sharing God's amazing grace that transforms hearts every day, and mends the broken pieces of our lives.

It is my prayer that the churches will place a genuine priority not only on sharing the good news of grace, but actually living in it. As long as we are part of a society that will forever be focused on what each and every one can amass for himself or herself, there will remain tremendous work left to be done on making sure anyone who is left behind finds a reason to live again, with the message that he or she is indeed worth fighting for.

The Church as an institution may become an instrument for this change and refine its guiding principles to continually reach out to people whose lives are often unintentionally, or even overtly, shoved to the edge of society. It is because we have been fortunate to receive the free gift of Christ's salvation, that we probably are in a unique position to go out into our communities with a message that touches lives rather than overlooking them. There will be individuals who walk through the church buildings and hallways over and again, whom not many of us pause even to recognize. If the people who walk in with disabilities can be so easily overlooked because we are preoccupied with our own lives, how much more those whose disabilities are disguised by their smiles and clothing?

Continuing Esi's story, I had been in touch with her ever since the Lord restored her and she had been active in reaching out to people who needed Christ. In April, 2018, around Easter time, I received a distressed call from her. What was happening again, I wondered. Esi had chanced upon Faustie, who was on the verge of dying and did not know what to do. Faustie, who was Esi's neighbor, had attempted an illegal abortion, and was bleeding to the point of death. Esi told Christie to accept Jesus and pray for forgiveness of sins, to help attract God's mercies on her life, but she blatantly refused. Esi later saw that her condition was becoming worse, so she took her to a private hospital. For some days, Faustie couldn't talk or eat and was in a coma. But all this while, Esi would call and we would pray for her.

On Good Friday, I asked my church to make an intercession for Faustie, for it is such persons that Jesus had come to die for. It was all joy when Faustie came back from her coma and later learnt that we had been praying for her. She was grateful to us that we did not let her die in sin, but rather took it upon ourselves to intercede on her behalf. The

Chapter 18: Worth Fighting For

same person who had once blatantly refused to accept Christ Jesus as her personal Savior, after gaining consciousness, admitted her sinful nature and accepted Christ to be her Lord. She was on admission for about two weeks, and all this while Esi was giving her the care she needed.

Though I was happy that God had given Faustie another chance to live and she had, this time round, accepted Jesus as her personal Savior, I became happier for Esi, when God chose her to save Faustie's life. Esi was declaring that Faustie would not die. Wasn't it amazing? She wanted her to live so that she would declare the works of the Lord. The one who had contemplated death, was now choosing life over death. Wasn't Esi worth fighting for?

Every child of God is worth fighting for, and the task of reaching out to the person next to us ought to be a sincere effort to do what Jesus would do: make them see again. When a church's constitution does not have any provision or specific programs that truly assist individuals who walk through their church doors with some physical or emotional disability, this leaves a void which the message of grace alone can fill.

A few years ago, a man pointed out something at the end of a church service. I knew what he was referring to and had been trying to galvanize some Church leaders to make a change, but that change had not come quickly enough. In the church's pews, a woman held on to a Bible tightly, but could not read anything in it. She was blind. There were no braille Bibles or hymn books for her. The man who brought the observation to my attention spoke about how he wished there were large print bibles for all the older people who were struggling to read the small text in the Bibles. These were minor hurdles for the church to address, but it spoke to a larger issue, and that was at the heart of what the man's observation led to.

In Ghana and across Africa, there may perhaps always be persons with hearing loss in our communities, but I am not sure how many of our churches make room for sign language resource persons to help them. Unfortunately, we seem, more often than not, to take our cues from the society around us, rather than becoming the ambassadors that God is counting on us to be. All of our lives are interconnected and how much God is counting on you and me, makes a difference. Every person, every heart, and every soul is worth fighting for.

By not stretching ourselves to bring hope to the men and women whose disabilities make them feel unwelcome, we are in fact reinforcing the prejudice that they are not worth our time and effort. Can God count on you and me to break the cycle that leaves more and more people every day on the wayside?

It is fascinating to imagine the scene unfolding: Jesus' encounter with a blind man in a community that was not ready to extend the same grace God extends to each and every one of us every day. Their attitude to the man may very well be the same as ours in contemporary society.

The congenitally blind man suffered discrimination, stigmatization, and rejection in his community. He was even stereotyped as a sinner by very religious people. The disciples who sat at Jesus' feet had a front row seat to grace, yet their vantage point had been colored by the society of which they had been a part all their lives.

The community in which the man found himself never handed him a good relationship because they tagged him as one that was born in sin. His encounter with Jesus shattered a stigma and inspires you and me to stand to action in the case of men and women whose conditions make it difficult to find their way in society. He was not a sinner, far from it. He was a friend to be loved, somebody's son. Jesus affirmed his innocence when he declared to the disciples that the man's blindness was to make the works of God become manifest in him.

The men and women in that Jewish community fought fiercely against what they thought was in opposition to their religious laws and their understanding of the Holy Scriptures. Would it have been a true testimony of the body of Christ if they had a different belief, one that said every soul was worth fighting for?

Often we assume someone else will take on that responsibility rather than taking a leap of faith to do the best that we can on our own, and praying that Almighty God will make provision for what we are unable to do. We may never find what brought people to the arenas of life in which they find themselves at a particular juncture, but that does not in any way negate the fact that they are also children of the Most High God and worth our love and our fight.

My prayer is that before we allow our own subconscious prejudices to make us tag individuals as sinners and unworthy, and find reasons to avoid them, let us all instead find our way to embrace the inconvenient truth about every man and woman whom God has fearfully and wonderfully made.

What can society do? Why does it often seem that even with the well-meaning legislation that local governments push for, the most important step of taking action falls apart at every turn, and nothing happens? Maybe, collectively, we have come to a point in our lives where we hope the law will solve every challenge. Rather I encourage a shift in our thinking, that the legislation is no more impactful a framework than the paper it is written on, if individuals like you and I do not take the initiative to make a difference in the communities we are a part of.

A simple question crossed my mind: What if politicians actually determine to enact laws to make it a little easier for a blind person to cross a road? What if the Church takes its message beyond the walls and the corridors into the communities in a sincere effort to touch lives? The standard that guides each one of our lives ought to transcend that of the politician whose job it is to help improve society. What guides us should be a heart that feels the pain of another wounded heart and seeks desperately to help them heal. Our standard ought to be God's standard. Our perspective ought to be God's.

There is nothing more fulfilling than fighting for a society where our objective, every day, is to see the world through God's eyes and not leave someone behind because of his or her physical, emotional or mental state.

When it comes to putting the needs of people with disabilities at the forefront of our agenda, everyone in his/her small way has a role to play. Can the world count on us to be the example of what it truly means to fight for people whose strength has taken them to the brink of a life that seems to be passing them by?

Our challenge is for Christ's power to be made evident in our lives, as intercessors to break loose the mental and physical chains that keep people from fulfilling what God has destined for them. The task is to restore the hearts of people to whom we are connected, and be the comforting hand to the society around us, to drum home that indeed everyone is worth fighting for. The resurrection power of Christ is still in the business of resurrecting broken hearts from the ashes of defeat and dejection. Can we stand in the gap and be counted on to be used by God?

In many more cases than we can imagine, we are surrounded by a cloud of witnesses watching what we will do. As Christians, as children of God, we are not slaves to social orientations and perspectives. Our salvation is a hefty enough price to extend that same grace to a hurting world, and find a reason in our heart to uplift someone whose plight may be different from our own, but to whom our smile and reaching out can make a lifetime of difference.

God looks for men and women who can be counted on. Will you and I be what He wants? Can you and I be inconvenienced long enough to step out of our comfort zones and reach out to someone, simply because he or she is worth fighting for? And we will do this because everyone, every man and woman both young and old, regardless of the physical or emotional hurdle that they have to overcome every day, is worthy.

Standing in the gap for our brother and sister who may be less fortunate than we are in one area of life or another is a cause worth fighting for. Note that, at one point or another in life we could be in a place where we too would need someone also to stand in the gap for us. If every person we come across is truly who Almighty God in His infinite wisdom has created him or her to be, I am convinced his or her life, no matter how fragile it is, is worth our sweat and fight.

My encouragement is that none of us would be so self-centered that the only thing in life that brings us a pain or a smile is that which concerns us alone. It would be tragic to have lived this life to its end, yet missed the golden opportunity to stand for another person.

In a world where all of us seem to be in a hurry to amass all the wealth we can, there will be so many people whom we would not have the chance to see, beyond the blur they have become. I truly hope that somewhere along our hasty way, we remember the people we run quickly past, some of who did not have the strength or the grace to plough through life like you and I may have.

Beyond the wall of our churches and the nests of our families, let us all be mindful of the truth that we cannot afford to give up on the next person's life, regardless of the station he or she finds himself or herself in at the present moment. There is no perfect excuse to discard a life that God has not given up on. It warms my heart to be reminded of the fact that some of the most inspirational stories in life, and the remarkable personalities who figure in those stories that many have heard about through the years, are the ones who arose out of the ashes of dejection and misery. When the world thought they were worthless and hopeless, somehow they stood again to finish the journey ahead of them.

What if we lived our lives every day with a heart that searches for a chance to uplift and inspire? What if we went through our next moments with the keen awareness that everyone we meet is handicapped in some form or fashion, desperate for a hand of grace to restore them? Perhaps some of the brightest days that another person experiences may come out of the hand we lend, as we latch on to the truth that no person is beyond the reach of grace. None of us would be where we are without grace. We all are indeed worth fighting for.

We are worth fighting for, not because we are perfect. Rather it is our imperfections that draw the best in all of our hearts and help us become all that we are created to be. It is my prayer and hope that the radiance of Christ's perfect love shines through all of our lives, one to another, for the world to see.

AFTERWORD

If there ever was a project of any great importance to a society and whose impact could have an incredible effect on every single person, this work is one of such. Using Ghana as a talking point, the case to honestly confront disability issues in communities around the world sounds a loud and urgent call to act. The issue of disability in society is one that cuts across the men and women whose plight is advertised or ignored.

This issue of disability is more than a charge to protect our elderly populations in societies where we easily abandon the men and women in their old age as if they have nothing else left to offer. In circumstances where society gives reasons to see a person as a burden on society, it is my hope that this work will spur in all of us the courage to rethink our own perspectives.

The premise of this book is incredibly simple: that with our willpower, there is almost nothing we cannot do that will make a lasting impact. But with the grace of Almighty God, we can begin the often difficult process of reshaping our own cultural values and outlooks.

As a researcher, I have found how the topic of disability is conveniently shelved to the side or to the corner, because we have determined as a society that we can afford to do so. From the boardroom to the religious leadership quarters and the high offices of political power, we seem to have all grown equally numb to the plight of our brothers and sisters.

Interestingly, we allow old traditions to dictate our views on disability in a way that we would never allow those same traditions to govern any other aspect of our thoughts and actions. Unfortunately, our attitude breaks the heart of many whose value is no less than our own and who by one reason or another have a different challenge than you and I.

Afterword

Can our society follow Jesus' example without being strapped by our own learned attitudes and cultural misconceptions? Can the church find the grace to genuinely seek to reach the hearts of the men and women who feel downtrodden and beaten down by diseases, failures, disappointments, rejection, and disability?

Truth is, our attitude can get in the way of God's agenda, especially when we are busy finding reasons why others, unlike us, live with one challenge or another. By his own example, Jesus opened a new and refreshing chapter to understanding disability.

One of the remarkably eye-opening encounters for me, was finding how many men and women with disabilities are not sitting in line waiting for anyone's sympathy or recognition as a charity case. There are many who have not resigned to their limitations and given up on themselves because they are blind, or persons with hearing loss, or have one form of disability or another. Consequently this book does not set out to make a case for pity. Rather, this project is to challenge every one of us to walk a proverbial mile in the shoes of our brothers and sisters to see the world from their vantage point, and then do the best we can to reevaluate our own perspectives.

As an editor of this book, I had the privilege of listening to countless stories from Rev. Joseph Cromwell from his own childhood, and I learned about some of the unimaginable hills he had to climb to be where he is today. His reality is one that I could not begin to fathom, but his story is one that I was convinced needed to be shared. I am particularly glad that he took a path that drives home the underlying message of grace.

I am of the opinion that this ought to be emulated by all Christians, and indeed society as a whole, to get closer, identify with, and advocate for persons with disabilities. We can only do this through a prism that is not blurred by social stigma and cultural behaviors, but one that has been made crystal clear through grace. It is only grace that changes everything.

E. Obeng-Amoako Edmonds

INDEX

A
Abundant grace
Admiratio populi
Anakites
Asiko Band
Asokore-Koforidua
Autism

C
Caleb
Canaan
Captain Foday Sankoh.
Celine Ebere Osukwu
Christian Council of Sierra Leone
Christological title
Congenital
Cultural attitudes

D
Diakonia
Disability
Disability-friendly

E
Ebun James
Edict
Eggli Silvia

G
"Gbiligbili"
Geneva
GHACOE Women's Ministry
Gilgal

H
Harold H. Wilke
Helakandah
Helen Keller

K
Kadesh Barnea
Kenizzite

L
Limuru
Ludwig van Beethoven

M
Mephibosheth
Merci mon ami
Messiahship
Moab
Murtala Muhammed Airport

N
National Union of Presbyterian Students-Ghana (NUPSG)
Nigeria Baptist Theological Seminary

O
Obafemi Awolowo University
Ogbomosho
Okorase
Order of Melchizedek
Orthodox and Catholic Churches
Oyo State

P

Paradigm shift
Pegasus Reef Hotel
Physical disability
Pool of Bethesda
Pool of Siloam
Potter's Hands
Promised Land

R

Revolutionary United Front (RUF)
River Asuoyaa
River Densu
Ruth

S

S. D. A. Teacher Training College
Sabbath
Sakyibea
Samuelson
Senior Eddie Donkor
Sheep Gate
Sisi
Son of David
Son of Man
Starfish
Synagogue
Sɛnea mete biara meyi me Nyame n'ayɛ

T

Taboo
Tamir tigers
Tanchara-Kunyukuo
The Torah
Theology of Diakonia
Thomas Kuhn
Tuscumbia, Alabama

U

U.S. Catholic Bishops on Persons with Disabilities
Unhealthy stereotypes
Union Theological Seminary
United Arab Emirates
United Nations Conventions on the Rights of Persons with Disabilities (UNCRPD)
University of Cape Coast
University of Haifa

W

West African Association of Theological Institutions (WAATI)
William Acquaah Cromwell
World Council of Churches (WCC)
World Health Organization (WHO)

At age two, with my brother William and sister, Janet. A few months later I became paralyzed after an injection from a local hospital.

With Jane and William on commissioning into the ministry at the Presbyterian Church of Ghana, Nativity Congregation, La, Accra. 2002

With Rev. Dr. Walter Altmann, Ms. Natalie Hendahewa, Mrs. Gertrude Oforiwa Fefoame, and Rev. Sunil Raj Philip at the Theology of Diakonia in the 21st Century Conference, in Colombo, Sri Lanka. 2012

Speaking at the 10th General Assembly of the All Africa Conference of Churches in Munyonyo Commonwealth Resort, Kampala, Uganda. 2013

With Rev. Dr. Andre Karamaga (former General Secretary of All Africa Conference of Churches - AACC) and Archbishop Valentino Mokiwa- President of AACC at the 10th General Assembly at Munyonyo, Kampala Uganda.

Attending church service in sixth-form at New Juaben Secondary Commercial School (NJUASCO), Koforidua, Ghana.

Graduated from the University of Cape Coast with Master of Philosophy in Religious Studies. 2015

As a student at seminary with the former President of Trinity Theological Seminary, Legon-Accra, Most Rev. Bishop Emmanuel K. Asante.

With my darling wife, Comfort, on our wedding day on 15 June, 2004.

We were privileged to have our marriage blessed by the then Moderator of the Presbyterian Church of Ghana, Rt Reverend Dr. Sam Prempeh, and his wife, Mama Adelaide Prempeh

I am forever grateful to God for this family.

As Associate Pastor with the Resurrection Congregation, Accra, participating in a Health Walk as part of its 120 year anniversary activities

With my parents Mr. Joseph Oliver Cromwell and Mrs. Joycetina Anyankwabea Cromwell, on my commissioning into ministry. 2002

Joseph Cromwell (fifth from left), first president of the "Jewels of His Crown" Choir, University of Cape Coast, Ghana

Damaged car from the train accident on the Abelemkpe-Alajo rail line

We are always thankful to God for saving us all in that terrible accident. 4 April, 2017

REFERENCES

Asiedu-Peprah, M. (2001). *Johannine Sabbath conflicts as juridical controversy.* Tubingen: Mohr Siebeck.

Barrett, C. K. (1978). *St. John: An introduction with commentary and notes on the Greek text.* London: SPCK.

Bauer, Walter (1957). A Greek-English lexicon of the New Testament: And other Christian literature. Chicago: The University of Chicago Press.

Braddock, D. L., & Parish, S. (2001). *An institutional history of disability.* Handbook of disability studies, 32(5), 565-574.

Brown, R. E. (1965). *New Testament Essays.* New York: Doubleday.

Brown, R. E. (1997). *An introduction to the New Testament.* New York: Doubleday.

Culpepper, A. (1983). *Anatomy of the Fourth Gospel:* A study in literary design. New York: Fortress Press.

Freed, E.D. (2001). *The New Testament:* A critical introduction. Belmont: Wadsworth.

Gal, J. (2001). *The perils of compensation in social welfare policy:* Disability policy in Israel. Social Service Review. 75 (2), 225-244.

Glover, B. X. (2013, April 29) *7 Communities abolish practice of killing infants with deformities.* Daily Graphic, p. 1,3.

Johns, L. L. & Miller, D. B. (1994). *The signs as Witness in the Fourth Gospel:* Re-examining the Evidence. The Catholic Biblical Quarterly. 56 (3), 519–535.

Johnstone, D. (2001). *An introduction to disability studies.* London: David Fulton.

Kysar, R. (1975). The Fourth Evangelist and his Gospel: An examination of contemporary scholarship. Minneapolis: Ausburg Publishing House.

Lindars, B. (1972). *The Gospel of John.* London: Oliphants.

Milington, P. (2006). *Ancient times: Sin, Religion and the body beautiful.* Timeline of disability history. Retrieved August 17, 2010

Moloney, F. J. (1998). *The Gospel of John*. Collegeville, Minnesota: The Liturgical Press.

Moulton, J. H. & Milligan, G. (1930). *The vocabulary of the Greek Testament*. Michigan: Grand Rapids.

O'Grady, J. F. (1989). *The Four Gospels and the Jesus tradition*. Mahwah, New Jersey: Paulist Press.

Osukwu, C. E. (2010, April-June). *The place of women with disabilities in Nigeria:* A paper presented at the International Day for Deaf Women in Nigeria in commemoration of International Women's Day 2010. Newsletter: Ecumenical Disability Advocates Network. (N/A), 12-15.

Otieno, P. O. (2009). "*Biblical and theological perspectives on disability:* Implications on the rights of persons with disability in Kenya." Disability Studies Quarterly, 29 (4).

Rimmerman, A. (2005). *Israel's equal rights for persons with disabilities Law:* Current status and future directions. Disability Studies Quarterly. 25, (4).

Speckman, M. T. (2007). *A biblical vision for Africa's development?* Pietermaritzburg: Cluster Publications.

Weiss, H. (1991). *The Sabbath in the Fourth Gospel. Journal of Biblical Literature.* 110 (2), 311–321.

Wenham, J. W. (1965). *The elements of New Testament Greek*. Cambridge: University Press.

Wilkie, H. H. (1979). Steps to Heaven. *Religion-online.* Retrieved October 08, 2010, from www.religion-online.org/showarticle.asp?title=1252.

"Wherever you are, be all there!
Live to the hilt every situation you believe
to be the will of God."

- Jim Elliot